DUEL IN THE HIGH TIMBER

"I'll part the hair of any son of a bitch that gets in my way!" Rufe shouted, holding the axe at port arms.

"Stand back!" Dave said, picking up the logging chain. His voice stopped the three or four men who had started forward.

It was an eight foot chain and he doubled it. Holding it by the center he whirled it around his head and began to advance...

Berkley Books by William O. Turner

A MAN CALLED JEFF
BLOOD DANCE
MAYBERLY'S KILL
THE SETTLER

WILLIAM O. TURNER

THE SETTLER

BERKLEY BOOKS, NEW YORK

THE SETTLER

A Berkley Book / published by arrangement with
the author

PRINTING HISTORY
Berkley edition / January 1977
Second printing / May 1982

All rights reserved.
Copyright © 1956 by William O. Turner.
This book may not be reproduced in whole or in part,
by mimeograph or any other means, without permission.
For information address: Berkley Publishing Corporation,
200 Madison Avenue, New York, New York 10016.

ISBN: 0-425-05605-8

A BERKLEY BOOK ® TM 757,375
The name "BERKLEY" and the stylized "B" with design
are trademarks belonging to Berkley Publishing Corporation.
PRINTED IN THE UNITED STATES OF AMERICA

1

DAVID PARTREY had got over the spine of the range into the fir forest of the western slope and into a cloud bank. Walking in front of his horse in the flowing fog, he tried to study out the trail in the duff. He was inexperienced at this and the tedium of it chafed him. When he blundered onto a spring with a trace of browse around it, he thought he might as well camp. He tethered the horse, gathered bark for a fire, and was crouching over his tinderbox when the Klikitats took him, closing their circle around him as silently as a drawn noose.

They were bucks from a small party that had come up behind him—six families on a late spring jaunt over the Cascades to trade with the Hudson's Bay Company, fish in the Sound, and steal horses from their brothers, the Nisquallies. They had first seen the rider ahead of them an hour earlier as he trotted across a glacial meadow near the summit of the pass. Amazed to see a lone white man on this high, grim trail that no one ever traveled alone, they held a brief council to discuss the possibility that he was a *tamanohus*, a spirit, in disguise. Were they not in the very shadow of the great mountain Tacoma, the abode of all *tamanohuses?* They could take no chances. Instead of shooting the stranger down at once, they would take him into custody until they were sure of his true nature.

Dave was too astonished to be frightened. He stood up slowly, turning to take in the full circle of his captors as they moved up somber and unreal, like nightmare creatures that would stare and threaten and drift back into the mist. They were dressed in white man's clothing filled out with blankets and buckskin. Several of them wore bright headbands that emphasized the unnatural slant of skulls flattened in infancy. Their fingers were on the triggers of old trade muskets.

Dave grinned at the nearest Indian. It was the reaction of a young man who had seldom been in the kind of trouble that a pleasant manner wouldn't get him out of. The Klikitat replied in Chinook, intertribal jargon of the Northwest. Dave had learned a few words at Fort Walla Walla and he wished now he had learned more. He supposed the Indian was asking who he was and where he was going.

"Boston tillicum," Dave said, pointing to himself. *Boston* was the Chinook word for any citizen of the United States. *Tillicum* meant friend. He made signs to indicate he was traveling westward.

Another Indian slipped forward to pick up Dave's carbine, then stepped close to unbuckle the flap of Dave's holster and lift out the new revolver he had bought and practiced with before leaving Illinois. This Indian wore a battered felt hat instead of a headband. A shiny twenty-five cent piece dangled from the lobe of each ear. He spat on the ground at Dave's feet and faced him arrogantly.

"I speak English. Howdy do. Where you going?"

"To the Sound," Dave said.

"What's your name?" He seemed to ask the question more to warm up his English than because of interest in the answer.

"David Partrey. What's yours?"

"White man can't say my Indian name. I got a name they call me. I tell you this name. It is Suchamuch."

"Glad to know you," Dave said dryly.

"You got whisky?"

Dave stepped back and got his saddlebags, took out a small flask of brandy and handed it to the Indian. Two others stepped up and took the saddlebags and began to go through them. Dave snatched them back. He took out some letters and slid them inside his shirt. He threw the saddlebags on the ground behind him and one of the Indians went around him and picked them up.

"What's them?" Suchamuch demanded after a long drink of the brandy. "Them papers."

"Letters. One of them is to the commander of the soldiers at Fort Steilacoom."

Suchamuch seemed impressed. He translated this information to the others, who were passing around the flask. An older Indian with a pockmarked face pushed up to take his drink and then stared closely at Dave as if he were nearsighted.

"This is the *tyee*, the chief," Suchamuch said. "Very stupid. He thinks you're some *tamanohus*, some damn spook."

"Tell him I'm just a Boston minding my own business."

"You bet. I tell him. After while he believe it.

Then we kill you. We kill you slow. What do the letters say?''

"They tell the soldiers who I am and why I am here."

"Why? Why you come here?"

"That's none of your business."

"You come to make a farm?"

"Yes," Dave said. "I come to make a farm."

"I think you lie. You say that like a lie."

"I'll tell you this, Suchamuch. The soldiers expect me. If I'm not at Fort Steilacoom in two days, they'll come looking for me." This was a long way from the truth, too, but Dave tried to make it sound convincing.

The rest of the party came up now, squaws and children and horses. The squaws threw their packs on the ground and began to gather wood for fires. A slender girl with a shawl over her shoulders came over and solemnly took the bark Dave had gathered. The young women were attractive enough, he thought, even though their skulls had been flattened more than those of the men.

"You got tobacco?" Suchamuch demanded.

Dave had three cigars in his pocket. He gave one to Suchamuch, another to the *tyee.* In an effort to appear at ease, he stuck the third between his teeth, went over to one of the fires and lit it on a twig. His saddlebags and saddle were gone. Several Indians were going through his rucksack and bedroll. He made no objection but picked up his mess kit and a sack of provisions and took them to the base of a tree, where he sat down, lazed back against the trunk and smoked. Two Indians came up and motioned that they wanted a puff. He had little choice but to oblige, hoping he was winning good will.

Suchamuch brought over an awkward boy of about fifteen who carried an ancient horse pistol a foot and a half long.

"This is your guard, Boston. You run, he kill you."

The boy sat against a tree a few feet from Dave, the pistol across his lap. In a way, these people were a comic-opera bunch, Dave thought, but the childishness that made them comic also made them deadly.

A cold wind had come up, thinning the mist. Darkness swiftly closed in on the camp. Followed by his guard, Dave scouted up wood and built himself a fire. He got bacon frying and a tin cup of water heating for tea.

The Indians were beginning to eat, passing around baskets of grayish boiled meat. One of the squaws had made a grill of stones and was cooking six-inch chunks of a large rattlesnake that she must have brought from the sagebrush country two or three days back. She had her fire somewhat off to itself and she sat alone, hooded in a blue army blanket. In a little while, she speared a chunk of the snake with a stick and brought it over to Dave's guard. She let the blanket fall to her shoulders and Dave saw that she was clean and pretty and her head wasn't flattened. She was plainly not a Klikitat.

The squaws had built their cooking fires in a rough circle. When they had finished eating, the Indian men gathered inside this circle, sitting on the ground, and held a council. Suchamuch rose to make the first speech. Several of the others spoke briefly. Even some of the squaws put in a word or two, not bothering to leave their fires.

It was clear enough to Dave that they were discussing him and that they couldn't decide what to do with him. The *tyee* and Suchamuch got into a heated argument. From gestures and intonations, it appeared that Suchamuch was in favor of killing him at once, while the *tyee* was against it. Suchamuch suddenly left the circle, swaggered over to Dave and stood over him with hands on hips.

"You got money, Boston?"

"A little."

"You give me money, I save you."

"How?"

"They all watch me talk to you. They don't know what we say. I tell them you got much *tamonohus*. You come here to talk to the Great Tamanohus of the mountain. I make them believe it."

Dave stood up, got out his purse, and gave the Indian a gold eagle. Suchamuch fingered the coin with affection and tucked it into the beaded bullet-bag that hung from his belt. He scowled.

"You give me the rest of that money. All of it."

"At Steilacoom. You get me out of here. Tonight. I'll see you at Steilacoom and pay you well."

"You give it to me now. Or you never see Steilacoom."

At the moment, it seemed to Dave that he had no choice but to hand over his purse. Suchamuch took it and examined it, as interested in the clasp as in the eighty dollars inside. He spat at Dave's feet and regarded him derisively. Too late, Dave realized that the man was cagily putting on a show for the others, proving that he could dominate the suspected *tamanohus*.

"You never see Steilacoom, Boston."

"You thieving little ape," Dave said softly. "You get me out of here right now or you'll hang within a week. I promise you that."

He moved a step toward the Indian and found himself looking into the muzzle of his own Colt. Out of the corner of his eye, he saw the boy who was guarding him stand up and cock his horse pistol.

"You want to start something?" Suchamuch said. "Come on. We kill you right now."

Suchamuch tossed his head in contempt, then abruptly turned his back and strode over to the council. He spat in Dave's direction and began to make a speech.

The squaw who had cooked the rattlesnake moved into the circle of fires, walking straight up to Suchamuch and waiting until he paused and faced her. Then she stuck out her chin and started to talk. She began calmly enough, but whenever Suchamuch opened his mouth to speak her words came louder and faster. Dave had never seen a man take such a tongue-lashing.

The Indians looked at one another uneasily, then seemed to listen with interest. Suchamuch was unable to get in a word. When he seized her wrist, she held the palm of her free hand close to his face and moved it back and forth in a strange sign which set the Indians to moaning. Suchamuch released her.

At last, hurling a drum-roll of gutturals at him, she backed him to the edge of the circle. She turned to the *tyee,* gestured toward Dave, and went on talking.

The *tyee* spoke briefly, apparently asking a question. They held a subdued conversation. The *tyee* spoke again, standing and addressing the others. He finished quickly and abruptly left the circle. The council was over.

The squaw marched to her fire, picked up a large chunk of baked snake and a knife, and came over and sliced off another piece for Dave's guard. She turned to Dave and smiled.

"They think I'm a witch. Isn't that ridiculous?"

He was completely confused at hearing her speak unaccented English. He scrambled to his feet and muttered something about her being as pretty a witch as he'd ever seen.

"This boy who has been guarding you killed the snake, so he gets some of it. Will you try it?"

He tasted it, found it delicious.

"You have tea," she said happily. "Will you brew me a cup?"

She sat down beside the fire, letting the blanket fall away from her shoulders. Under it she wore a doeskin jacket with circles of blue beads over her breasts. Beaded moccasins protruded from under her voluminous wool skirt.

"Now you listen to me, mister. It's all right; they'll let you go. But don't be in a hurry about it. Don't act scared. They'll bring back the things they took from you. Wait till you have them all, then quietly pack up and hightail it out of here."

"What did you tell them?" Dave asked.

She smiled deliciously. "I said everything that came into my head. Indians are like children. They're afraid of the dark, so I talked about ghosts and devils and such. Of course, that Suchamuch didn't swallow it. I doubt if you get back the money you gave him. And it's just possible he'll sneak away and follow you. So keep going. Don't camp tonight."

"I don't know how to thank you," Dave said. "If I can help you in any way—"

"Of course you can. Do you think I saved your skin just because I like your baby-blue eyes? Who do you think I am? Pocahontas?"

He grinned. "I think you're a witch."

"You can get more money at Steilacoom, can't you? . . . Well, you can give me enough for a new shawl and a pair of shoes."

From a squaw who spoke like an educated white woman, this seemed a strange request, but Dave didn't say so. After a moment he laughed.

"I was just thinking," he said. "When I get back to Illinois, I'll tell about this supper—tea and rattlesnake—and nobody will believe me."

"Listen," she said. "Tea and rattlesnake and a beautiful witch!"

They sat and talked and got acquainted. The Indians began to bring back Dave's outfit, piling it an item at a time a little to one side of the fire. He and the squaw paid them no attention. She was glad to have someone to talk to and told him all about herself.

Her name was Sally Sugar and she was half white, the daughter of two halfbreeds. Her mother's Indian blood was Shoshone. She wasn't sure what her father's was. He was born somewhere south of St. Louis and she thought he might be Choctaw. He had come to Oregon to buy furs for old John Jacob Astor's American Fur Company and he had met her mother on the way.

"I think his name was Sugrue," Sally said, "but they called it Sugar at the mission. Mother took me every day to the mission to school. The Whitman mission. They let her go to school too. We stayed up half the night getting our lessons letter-perfect. Mother lived only for me. She wanted me to have a chance at a decent life.

"When I got older, I helped teach the small children. I loved it. When Father died, Mother and I moved to the mission. You've heard of the massacre. We were there. One of the Cayuse Indians was in love with me and he protected us and put us on horses and we got away. Afterward, we went back. We saw the bodies. Twelve bodies."

Dave stirred the fire so he could see her more clearly. *She's the prettiest girl this side of St. Louis,* he thought.

"The soldiers came then and built Fort Walla Walla. I married a lieutenant. Mother died that same year. She died happy; she believed I was taken care of. Three years ago, my husband was transferred back east. He wouldn't take me. He said we weren't legally married.

"Last week, a soldier who had been to Fort Steilacoom said he'd seen my husband in the town there. In civilian clothes. So I asked these filthy pinheads, these Klikitats, to take me over the mountains with them." She shrugged. "It's a small chance that he'll take me back, even if he's there. But what else can I do? What is there for an Indian except to be a servant or a slut?"

The *tyee* came over and laid Dave's rifle among the returned plunder. He spoke to Sally, who acted as interpreter.

"He says that Suchamuch insists on keeping your revolver and your money. He is angry at Suchamuch for this. He hopes you will think well of him and speak a good word for him to the Great Tamanohus and also to the white soldiers at Fort Steilacoom. . . . Now say a few words in return, with gestures."

Dave stood up and spoke very soberly. "Tell him I believe it in his best interest to keep this whole affair a secret from the Great Tamanohus but I will certainly mention him to the soldiers. And if that isn't the right thing to say, my most beautiful of witches, why, make up something."

Sally purred a string of Chinook at the Indian and he seemed highly pleased. He shook hands with Dave, white-man fashion, and left them.

Dave began to sort and pack his possessions. Sally sat and watched. The Indians raked all their fires into one big one and bedded down around it, choosing the warmed places and shaping the duff to fit their bodies. The guard left his post and bedded down with the others. A star sparkled through the treetops.

"Now!" Sally said, when Dave's blankets were rolled and his rucksack filled. "Go as quickly and unobtrusively as possible. If Suchamuch tries to stop you, I'll get the *tyee*."

"Will you be all right?"

"I'll be fine. I'll see you at Steilacoom, Mr. Partrey."

Dave loaded himself with saddle, saddlebags, bedroll and rucksack. Before he started off toward the place where his horse was tied, he paused beside Sally to say: "I forgot. At Steilacoom, I'll be known as Porter—David Porter."

2

FINDING THE WAY in the thick forest night was at first as tense a business as in the cloud bank; then Dave discovered he could trust the hard-mouthed little gelding he had traded for at Walla Walla. As blind as its rider in the fog, the animal could follow a trail in darkness.

Shortly after dawn, Dave came out of the trees onto a rocky slope where there was a sudden view of the great white mountain, unbelievably near, stained with the last blue shadows of night and the first frail rose of day. In spite of his haste, he halted to marvel at the sight, to feel its great tranquillity without quite accepting it. It wasn't real. To a man who had always known the soft rich prairieland of Illinois, the mountain wasn't real even while he stared at it.

The trail, steep and rock-slippery, led down the chine of a ridge to a wooded valley. Here the great firs shared the ground with cedar, maple, oak, alder. Briars and brush grew in a tangle with vine maple, ferns, nettles and fallen trunks; a man couldn't have walked three yards off the trail without an axe.

Dave heard the churning of a river minutes before he came to it, a clear mountain stream that soon joined another and became a milky gray. Near the junction, he had to make a crossing in swift water up to his horse's belly. On the far bank he found an open space, an old burn carpeted with grass, and he paused briefly for breakfast. If Suchamuch was close on his heels, Dave thought, he would see the Indian fording the river and would be ready for him; but he saw no one.

Before the day was over, he had to cross the frothy S'Kamish River some twenty times, getting soaked more than once when his horse lost its footing. The trail continued to be a sunless tunnel and he had no chance to get dry. At last it veered away from the river and widened into a road marked with fresh black ruts. An hour after sundown he came to a clearing in which there stood a cabin and a lean-to with a cow stabled under it.

The place turned out to be occupied by a middle-aged Englishman and his plump young squaw. He was delighted to have company and Dave stayed the night here, dining on venison and sitting late over a jug of wild raspberry wine while his host extolled the future of northern Oregon.

Although there were now fewer than two hundred white families in the whole area north of the Columbia, the Puget Sound country was on the verge of a boom, the Englishman said. He based this prediction mostly on the fact that the Army planned to build a road over the Naches pass, following the trail Dave had just come over.

"Wagon trains pour into Oregon by the score, but we get precious few settlers up here," he explained. "They go down the Columbia to Oregon City and the other settlements down there. The Naches road will bring them directly to us."

"You'll have neighbors," Dave said. "Will you like that?"

The man chuckled. "I'll move farther back in the woods."

"Speaking of neighbors," Dave said, trying to sound casual, "is there a family around here somewhere named Covey?"

"Covey? I've heard the name. They're near the Puyallup, I think, but I can't say precisely where. Ten or twelve miles southwest of here, I should think. Almost my nearest neighbors at that."

"How large a family are they?"

"Man and wife and three or four children. Oldest girl's a bit of a charmer."

"Anyone else living with them? A relative or hired man or anyone like that?"

"I don't know of anyone. There might be though. Are you looking for somebody?"

"In a way," Dave said guardedly. "It isn't important."

He had had no sleep for thirty-six hours and he slept late in the morning. He had another two hours of forest travel, then the road flowed onto a vast grassland that rolled away toward distant foothills and the great cloud-capped mountain. This was the Nisqually plain, where the Indians had for generations burned back the forest to make a feeding ground for deer.

In the middle of the afternoon, he reached Fort Steilacoom, a mile and a half inland from the town. A detail of red-undershirted soldiers were repairing the palisade of fir poles that surrounded the area. Dave questioned the sentry at the gate and, following directions, rode past a row of log barracks to a frame building opposite the parade ground. He was received by a sleepy-eyed sergeant and promptly ushered into the office of the commanding officer.

"I have orders regarding you," Captain Maloney said, shaking hands cordially and waving Dave to a chair. He jerked open a desk drawer and brought out a sheaf of papers and two black cigars. He cupped a sulphur match for Dave, sprang the papers off his thumb and extracted one. "Here they are. They're a bit unusual, but clear enough. You bring in your man and the Army will get him back to the States for you. We'll relay him from post to post all the way to Illinois."

Dave was pleased. "It's good to know that those orders are already here. I was afraid there'd be delay."

"I also have a letter from the Governor of Oregon to be delivered to you. It's addressed to all territorial officials and directs them to co-operate with you. Could be mighty useful." The captain passed the letter to Dave, who glanced at it, returned it to its envelope, and slid it into his pocket.

"This Bart Hadder you're after is a convicted murderer," the captain said. "Is that correct?"

"He killed my brother."

Captain Maloney looked surprised. "That explains a lot. How did it happen?"

"Hadder was trying to swindle a friend of my

brother's, trying to get him to invest in a large piece of property that the Illinois Central Railroad was supposed to want. My brother got suspicious. He investigated and found that Hadder was a riverboat card shark and confidence man and that the railroad already owned the land Hadder was trying to sell. Hadder killed him to keep him from warning his friend."

Dave paused and puffed on his cigar. It was strong and foul but it was the first he had had in two days and it put him in a mellow mood.

"Hadder was sentenced to hang?" the captain asked.

"Yes. He killed a guard and escaped while he was being moved to the penitentiary. The state trailed him to California. The man who followed him there reported that he had shipped on a tramp schooner and was out of the country. At that point, the state gave up the chase.

"In the meantime, I'd done a little nosing around on my own and I had a hunch Hadder might head for Oregon. I got the idea from talking to a former gambling partner of his who had quarreled with him and who now hates his guts. He said Hadder was always talking about the forests out here and dreamed of coming and making a fortune out of timber.

"At first, it was just a hunch. Then word came from San Francisco that Hadder's ship had returned there—without him, of course. Several of the crew had jumped ship at one port and another and the captain wasn't sure where he had lost the man answering Hadder's description. But, among other places, the ship had been to Puget Sound.

"Finally, I looked up Hadder's family and learned that an older sister has settled out here. She's the only close relative he has and the one he would probably go to if he needed money. Her married name is Covey. You may know the family."

Captain Maloney squinted at the ceiling. "Covey? I think I've heard the name. But I can't tell you where they're located. Not offhand."

"It seemed to me a pretty safe bet that Hadder's around Puget Sound somewhere and I tried to get the state to put a man on his trail again, but they wouldn't do it. So I went to the governor and told him I was going to find Hadder on my own. He didn't like the idea of a murdered man's brother going after the murderer; but when he saw he couldn't stop me, he gave me what help he could without giving me official recognition."

Captain Maloney studied the orders again, shifting his cigar across his face. "Well, he got the Army to co-operate with you. And the Governor of Oregon Territory."

"I suspect that's partly the work of an ex-Congressman I know back in Springfield," Dave said. "Man named Lincoln."

"Well, the main thing is to be careful," Maloney said. "I don't want to have to write a report about how we found your body in the woods or washed up on a beach. You're after a desperate man—that's plain. And there are our Indians. I'll wager you don't know the first thing about our Indians."

"I've already had a brush with them. I came as far as Fort Hall with a big party and we hardly got a close look at an Indian all the way. Then a bunch of them caught up with me coming over the Cascades." Dave found himself telling about his capture as if it were highly amusing.

Captain Maloney listened closely. "Those were Klikitats, all right," he said when Dave had finished. "Not Puget Sound Indians. You were lucky to get away in one piece. A favorite trick of theirs is to skin a man alive. I know that Suchamuch. He grew up at the Hudson's Bay post six miles south of here."

"Is there any chance of my getting my revolver and my money back?" Dave asked. "I'm traveling at my own expense, as you know."

"I'll send out a detail to intercept that party and bring it in. I'll do it right now."

The captain left the room and Dave could hear him giving orders to the sergeant. In a moment he was back. He handed Dave a paper covered on both sides with columns of words written in a meticulous hand.

"That's a Chinook vocabulary. Only three hundred words in the whole language and you can learn it in a week if you work at it. It will be worth it if you have to deal with Indians. Our Sound Indians are mostly peaceful enough, though a few individuals are dangerous. You can usually talk your way out of trouble—if you can speak Chinook."

The captain invited Dave to spend the night on the post, but Dave turned him down. "I'll get a room in town if I can—preferably with a feather mattress."

"I don't blame you," Captain Maloney said. "But don't expect too much. It's not much of a town."

He followed Dave to the wide porch that overlooked the parade ground. "Tell me—what if this Hadder sees you first?"

"I have an advantage there. I saw him at the trail, so I'll recognize him easily enough. But he doesn't know me. Of course he'd recognize my name. That's why I'm changing it to Porter. David Porter."

Steilacoom consisted of some thirty buildings, log and frame, scattered along muddy streets on a slope above the Sound. Dave got his first view of salt water here. Riding straight downhill to the lowest street, Commercial, he looked across a current-streaked bay to darkly timbered islands. Two sailing ships were anchored just offshore, loading logs from rafts. A smaller vessel was tied up at a dock. A long, two-story building with a sagging roof stood half on the dock, half on shore. Over the door was a sign burned into a board with a poker:

BALCH AND WEBBER
GENERAL MERCHANDISE
BANK AND POST OFFICE
LOGS AND SQUARE TIMBER
CHOICE LOTS FOR SALE

Dave tied his horse and went in. A bearded, youngish man in shirt sleeves and waistcoat was putting eggs into a basket for a woman. "Still a dollar a dozen," he said. The woman paid him and went out.

"Are you Captain Balch?" Dave asked.

"I am that."

Dave presented a draft made out to David Porter for two hundred dollars, all the money he had in the world. It was on an Oregon City bank for which Balch was agent.

"I'd like to draw a hundred now and leave the rest in your keeping until I need it."

Lafayette Balch was a Scot, a former sea captain. He had a pleasant manner and a handsome face with a shrewdness about his little black eyes. He alternately studied Dave and the draft for some time before leading the way back to a cluttered office, where he got the money out of an iron-bound chest. He counted ninety dollars in gold into Dave's hand.

"My fee is ten per cent," he explained.

Dave bought half a dozen cigars, two blue-checked shirts and a cake of shaving soap. Chatting casually with the storekeeper, he learned that the store was built of New England lumber—Balch had built it in sections in Boston, loaded it on a ship, and brought it around the Horn. He'd sailed up and down the West Coast looking for a place to put up his store and had picked Steilacoom. "That was better than two years ago," he said. "Nothing here at all then—except a sawmill!"

Dave took his horse to a livery barn and followed a springy boardwalk back to a hotel almost across the street from Balch's. It was a red building with white trim and a white-railed balcony built out over the walk. A bell jangled as he entered a small parlor, and a red-faced woman bustled in from another room. She took him upstairs to a large clean room with a braided rug on the floor, a fireplace and a view of the water.

He asked for a pitcher of hot water and while the landlady went for it, he stood in the double window and fed on the tranquillity of the Sound. The landlady startled him when she set the pitcher in the china washbasin. "Supper in an hour," she said.

Dave washed, shaved, and put on one of the new shirts. He went back to the window to watch the sun sink behind the haze-blue islands across the passage.

The first part is over and done with, he thought. *I got here. The next part will be to find Bart Hadder without alarming him and to take him into custody. I'll take him or kill him or get killed. One way or another, I'll get that over and done with, too, and as soon as I can. Then, if I'm alive, I can rest. Maybe I'll come to this room and rest for a week.*

He found supper an unremarkable meal served to a room-long table of boarders by the landlady and two husky German girls. Afterward he walked around the town, finding the twisted streets quiet—except for Commercial, which was now busy with men going in and out of Balch's and the log saloons. Dave had a drink in each of these, paying ten cents a glass for weak whisky that tasted of prune juice and looking over the card games. Wherever Bart Hadder was, it was a safe bet that he spent most of his time at a card table.

Back at the hotel, the landlady gave Dave a note from Captain Maloney, which he took to the privacy of his room to read.

Mr. David Porter
Sir:

My men brought in the Klikitats, who were only about three hours behind you. Suchamuch was not with them. I suspect he slipped away as soon as he saw soldiers approaching. I gave the rest of the group a lecture about intercepting white travelers and am detaining them tonight, letting them camp outside the palisade, under guard. I will inform their big tyee, *Owhi, who is currently on this side of the mountains, of the incident and will request that he administer punishment.*

You will perhaps be glad to learn that my clerk knows of a Covey family (Isaac F. Covey) which occupies a donation claim near the Puyallup River and which is very likely the family you are seeking. I have had him make a map showing the exact location and I enclose this for your guidance.

Very resp. yr. obdt. srvt.,
M. Maloney
Capt. Artillery, Command-
ing
Postscript: That Sally-squaw said she was in a hurry to get to Steilacoom and I let her go.

M. M.

3

THE NEXT MORNING the town of Steilacoom hummed with sensational news: northern Oregon had been made a Territory in its own right!

Washington, this northwest corner of the United States was to be called—Washington Territory. The bill had been passed by Congress and signed by President Fillmore only a few days after Dave left Illinois. The news had trailed him across the country, never quite catching up with him but sweeping past him on the last leg of his journey and going down the Columbia to Portland. From there it had been brought up the Cowlitz trail to Olympia, the new territorial captial, and on to Steilacoom. It would be borne to Port Townsend and to New York Alki, the other settlements on the Sound, by Murphy's Indian Canoe Express.

Dave heard it when he entered the dining room for breakfast and two of the boarders shouted it at him at once. The meal turned out to be a celebration, with a stone flask making the rounds when the landlady wasn't looking.

"A gr-r-rand historical moment it is," said a gray-bearded Irish sea captain who had freely laced his coffee with whisky. "It means the proper development of the gr-r-reat area with the seat of government on the Sound instead of the thither side of the Columbia."

Dave passed up the whisky, but found he was pleasantly elated by the news. It gave him a sense of participation in something important, and he had to remind himself he was just a visitor, an onlooker.

When he went into the street, he found a crowd gathered in front of Balch's store, where Balch was making a speech from the doorway. He listened a moment and gathered that Balch had been one of the leaders in the movement to separate from Oregon. During one of the frequent outbursts of cheering, he asked a man on the outskirts of the crowd to direct him to the sheriff's office, which turned out to be some little distance up the hill in a section apart from the lower town.

The sheriff was sick. The deputy in charge of the office was drunk. He glanced at Dave's letter from the governor and tossed it on the desk.

"Hell fire!" he sputtered, grinning idiotically. "This paper don't mean nothin'. This ain't Oregon no more and anything that says Oregon on it ain't no damn good—not in this office!"

"Well," Dave said patiently, "I'm looking for a criminal who has relatives on a farm in the Puyallup valley. I'm going out to see if he's there. Will you send a deputy with me?"

"Ain't you man enough to go by your own self?"

"He's a desperate man. He's more likely to surrender peaceably to two men than to one."

The deputy snorted and tilted back in his chair. He was a fat man on a small frame; he seemed to be all stomach.

"I ain't goin'. I'm the only deputy and I got to take care of town. Go a-ridin' off into the country and folks would say I was gone on a drunk."

"Can you deputize somebody to go with me."

"I don't think I can do that. Ain't got the authority. It takes the sheriff to do that."

"Where will I find him?" Dave demanded.

"He's got cholera and he's so sick he don't recognize his own wife. He ain't likely to come through it."

"The Puyallup valley is in your county, isn't it? It seems to me to be your duty to give me some help."

" 'Seems to you' don't count, sonny. If you wasn't a yellowback, you'd git your man your own self."

"All right," Dave said softly. "The hell with you. Just remember I asked you."

He left the building, walked back to the hotel for his carbine, got his horse at the livery barn and rode out of Steilacoom. Guided by Maloney's map, he followed the road he had come into town on. When he was well into the timber, he turned northeast into a bough-choked fork that he hadn't noticed the day before.

He reached the Covey farm about noon, glimpsing a small unpainted house and a large log barn through the foliage before he reached the clearing. Tying his horse, he left the road and made his way on foot through the brush to a place where he could watch the house without being seen.

There were nine or ten acres of cleared land, about half of it in pasture and the rest in wheat and potatoes. A cow, a saddle horse and two oxen grazed in the pasture. A boy about twelve was hoeing a vegetable patch between the house and the long log barn.

After a few minutes, a young woman in a green-checked apron came to the door of the house and called to the boy, who went to the barn and called to some one inside. The boy then strode to the low back porch, sloshed water from a bucket into a tin basin, washed his hands and face, and went into the house. A man with a thatch of gray hair came from the barn to the porch and went through the same routine.

The man was not Bart Hadder and Dave watched a while longer to be sure no one else was in the barn. Then he got his horse and rode up to the house. The family was plainly at lunch. If Hadder was there, he would in all probability be at the table and it would be easy enough to cover him.

The door opened and the girl in the checked apron stepped onto the porch, a lithe, well-formed girl with blond braids wrapped prettily around her temples.

She said, "Oh," as if she were expecting someone else. Then, smiling, she said, "How d'you do."

"I'm lost," Dave said. "I'm out of provisions and badly in need of a meal."

"Well, you got here just right. We're just at dinner."

A woman's voice called from inside, "Is it Holland?"

"Come in," the girl said. "No, Mother, it's somebody else. Man who's lost."

He tied the reins to one of the posts that supported the porch roof, tucked his carbine under his arm and stepped into the kitchen. There were five people at the table: the man and boy he had seen outside, two little girls, and a woman with gray-streaked hair and a haggard face. Bart Hadder was not there. The man stood up and extended his hand across the table.

"My name's Isaac Covey and these here are my family. Welcome to you, sir, and please to accept of our hospitality."

"That food smells good," Dave said, nodding to Mrs. Covey.

"I'm Alice," one of the little girls said. "Pleased to meetcha."

"I'll get you a chair to set on," Isaac Covey said, going into the front room.

Dave followed him. It seemed unlikely that there was anyone else in the house but he was glad of a chance to make sure. Two small bedrooms opened off the living room. The doors were open and Dave moved to where he could see into them. They were empty. Covey looked at him inquisitively.

"I'm looking for a place to put my gun—where the youngsters won't bother it," Dave said.

"Stand it in a corner of the kitchen. They know better than to touch it."

Dave sat down to a meal of white beans boiled with chunks of ham and served on thick slices of bread. It was tasty fare, there was a great pot of it, and he ate as if his story about being lost and out of provisions were true.

The Coveys hadn't heard the news about the new Territory and he found himself telling it, risking their suspicion if they were to learn that the report had reached Steilacoom only that morning.

After their excitement had died down, Mrs. Covey questioned him about himself. He said he was looking over the country around the Sound with a view to taking out a claim for a farm.

"The land around here is no good," Mrs. Covey said. "It's too hard to clear." Looking straight at her husband, she added, "At least, it's too much for Ike."

"Well, I don't know," Isaac Covey said. "I allow I'd as soon clear a place in the Pit, but I think I've done pretty well. I've hacked out ten acres in three years and farmed at the same time. Mr. Porter could do as well."

"As well!" Mrs. Covey said acidly. "Everything you own is mortgaged!"

"Don't discourage Mr. Porter," the girl who had admitted Dave said. She was about eighteen or nineteen and her name was Ann. "It would be a grand thing to have a neighbor."

Dave turned to Mr. Covey. "How about that land around Steilacoom? That prairieland."

"The Hudson's Bay Company lays claim to every last inch of that. Claims the treaty of '46 with Britain give 'em the whole of it."

"There's a fine piece of land next to us," Ann said. "It lies right in the bend of the river."

"Ann!" Mrs. Covey said. "That land belongs to Holland Gay." Turning to Dave, she said with unnecessary emphasis. "Holland Gay is the man Ann is to marry."

"Mother, please. Don't tell it like it was a settled thing. I haven't said I'll marry him."

"He wants you—we know that. And you take to him too. Don't you deny to it!"

"I haven't made up my mind."

"That *is* a pretty piece of land in the river bend," Isaac Covey said. "Sometimes I wish I'd claimed it instead of this here."

"Holland has *not* claimed it," Ann said. "He likes it, all right, but he can't claim it without giving up the claim he's already got on Fox Island. He built a cabin on that one but he don't even live on it the way he's supposed to. He lives in Steilacoom."

"He's a Steilacoom businessman," Mrs. Covey said.

"He owns a saloon," Ann said, getting up to refill Dave's coffee cup.

"I'll take a look at that land," Dave said.

"I know something about that place that I've never told anyone," Ann said.

"What?" Mrs. Covey demanded.

"I'm not going to tell."

"Well," Isaac Covey said to Dave, "you go and give it a look-over and then come back here and take supper and the night with us. There's a bunk in the barn my brother-in-law built. T'ain't fancy but you'll be comfortable enough."

"Yes. Fine. Thank you very much," Dave said, hoping his voice didn't betray his excitement. *Covey's brother-in-law!*

"You have relatives out here?" he asked.

"Just Hannah's brother Ben. He drops in on us to spend a few days every now and again."

"Is he a farmer?"

"Ben? He's in the lumber business, I guess you'd say, wouldn't you, Hannah?"

"Yes, in a manner of speakin', it's the lumber business."

"At Steilacoom?" Dave asked.

"All over," Mrs. Covey said. "He travels around to the mills all over the Sound. There must be eight or ten of them he visits. I sure wish Ike would get into lumber. That's where the money is—not in farmin'."

"It'll be in farmin' too. You'll see," Isaac Covey said. "When the wagons start a-rollin' in here and the country gets settled up—"

He launched into a glowing prophecy of the future of farming in the Puyallup valley. Dave would have liked to switch the conversation back to Mrs. Covey's brother, but he didn't see how he could do it without being suspiciously inquisitive. Brother "Ben" was Bart Hadder; he had no doubt of that. That he was here, in the Sound country, was no longer a conjecture. He traveled around to the mills. Dave wondered what his assumed name was: Ben what? If he stayed the night, he thought, he might get a chance to question one of the kids.

When they got up from the table, he asked the way to the river bend, got his hat and gun, and went out to his horse. Ann Covey followed him.

"Why don't you turn him into the pasture?" she

said, laying her palm on the gelding's nose. "I'll walk with you, show you the way."

When they had left the pasture gate and started along the edge of the wheat toward the woods, Mrs. Covey called to Ann from the porch.

"I'll be right back, Mother!" Ann called over her shoulder. To Dave she said, "I call her Mother because she asked me to. She's really my stepmother. Mine and Bobby's. The girls are hers."

He was glad Ann was going to be in an informative mood. He began to think of ways to lead the conversation around to her step-uncle Ben.

"This country can be hard on a woman," Ann said. "It's made Mother peevish. Everything you do, you feel her watching and criticizing in her mind, even when she don't say anything. She keeps everybody on edge—'specially my father."

"You've been here three years?"

"Yes. We crossed from St. Louis in '49 and lived a year in Oregon City. Bobby and I went to school there. I worry about Bobby because he's getting no schooling here. I got seven years altogether, but he's had only a year and a half and is getting no more. I try to teach him but he isn't interested. A boy needs schooling worse than a girl."

"Don't you get lonesome here?"

"Oh, sure. But you get used to it. About the only visitors we have are Injuns. We feed them when they come around and we get along fine with them. And there's Holland Gay."

"The man you're to marry."

"Don't you bet any money on that."

The woods were dark. The trail was ragged with brush and branches. Dave's hand smarted from a nettle sting. Ann swept gracefully ahead, taking her position as guide very seriously.

"How about your uncle—the one in the lumber business?" Dave asked. "Does he visit you often?"

"Uncle Ben? He comes here every once in a while. He comes here to drink. He gets drunk and lies out in the barn all day. I don't like to go near him. Once he stayed sober and he was lots of fun. He did some card tricks for us and I don't see how he did them."

This fitted to a T the picture Dave had gleaned of Bart Hadder. Big, curly-haired Bart Hadder who went off by himself to do his drinking. Bart Hadder the card shark, the vain expert who couldn't resist the temptation to show off his skill.

"What's his last name?" Dave asked, too abruptly.

Ann didn't answer for a moment. She paused to hold back a branch for Dave, giving him an appraising glance.

"Well, I don't rightly know. I can't remember hearing anything but 'Ben.' I do know he changed his name because he got in some kind of trouble, I don't know what. I'm not supposed to talk about it."

She moved along the trail again, but without talking; Dave was afraid he had aroused her suspicions. They were getting close to the river and could hear the roar of the current, so steady he was hardly aware of it. All the little sounds of birds and wind were smothered and, unless Dave reminded himself to hear the roar itself, the woods seemed a place of unearthly silence.

They came suddenly into the sunlight and were at the bend, where a rocky point lay between them and the churning water. Two Indians were fishing at the point and Ann spoke to them in Chinook. They had caught several large salmon that lay in the shade at the edge of the woods.

"Are you really looking for a claim?" Ann said, again looking at Dave appraisingly.

"Certainly."

"Well, this would be a corner of your land if you took one here. The river would be your boundary on two sides. How old are you?"

"Twenty-five."

"That's just old enough. Isn't it?"

"For what?"

"For taking out a claim under the Oregon Land Law. Didn't you know that?"

"Of course," Dave said. "I didn't know what you were talking about."

"How many acres are you allowed? Do you know that?"

"Of course. A hundred and sixty."

"That's under the old Pre-emption Act. You can get three hundred and twenty under the Oregon Law if you file before December first of this year."

"So much the better."

"How many acres can a man and wife take? Do you know that?"

"No," he admitted.

"Six hundred and forty. You don't know much about taking out a claim."

"I haven't been in Oregon long," he said lamely.

She was suspicious—he could see that. She surely didn't know the true reason Uncle Ben had changed his name; probably none of the Coveys knew it, or they wouldn't have mentioned him at all. But she suspected, vaguely and without being at all sure about it, that Dave was pursuing Uncle Ben and was not interested in land.

He decided to go through the motions of taking out a claim here—that ought to dismiss her doubts about him once and for all. Besides, a claim near the Coveys would give him an excuse to keep in touch with them, to pick up more information about Uncle Ben, to watch for a visit from him.

"I like this land," he said, facing the woods. "It will be a jungle to clear but I guess it's no worse than other places. I like the idea of being on a river."

"If you decide to take it, I'll tell you the secret I know about it."

"All right—I've decided."

She was pleased. "It's something I'll have to show you. There's a trail along the river that will take us near it."

One of the Indians came up to them, making guttural noises. Dave made out the words *tyee salmon*.

"He has caught a great chief of the salmon," Ann said. "He wants to sell him to you."

"Can you use it?"

"It would be nice for supper. Otherwise you'll probably get beans again."

Dave took some coins from his pocket but the Indian shook his head at money. They settled on a price of five bullets and five charges of powder, measured from Dave's powder flask. Dave shoved a stick through the lower jaw of the thirty-inch fish to carry it by.

They took the river trail with Ann again leading the way, sometimes along the bank, sometimes descending to a few yards of narrow beach. They hadn't gone far when she paused beside two fir saplings growing close together.

"We leave the trail here. The going will be scratchy for a while," she said and disappeared between the trees.

For perhaps two hundred yards they pushed through brush, climbed over vine maple, walked a fallen trunk across a slough.

"Here it is!" Ann said, picking her way through a clump of alder and stepping into a sunny meadow completely hidden in the forest. It was covered with ankle-deep grass and was free of trees except for a pair of oaks near its center and a few fir saplings of Christmas-tree size. It was at least four acres in area—four acres that wouldn't have to be cleared.

"Nobody knows about this?" Dave asked incredulously.

"Sometimes I think Father has found it and has said nothing because Mother would be upset it isn't on our place."

"Your friend—Holland Gay. Does he know?"

"No." She stuck out her chin as if defying him to be surprised.

This place has a cash value, he thought. *Not much maybe, but something. I'll file on it, build some sort of cabin, and then sell my rights.*

"Do you like it?" she asked expectantly.

"Of course I like it. I'm grateful to you."

A bright green snake slid through the grass and raised itself to look at Ann. She kicked at it and said "Shoo!" and it darted away. They laughed and she moved closer to him and their eyes met and they grew sober.

"It will be nice to have you for a neighbor," she said. "Somebody young."

She was a stately girl, straight and graceful, and her braids wreathed her head like a pale coronet. Her eyes were brown and they held his steadily. She was a girl who could be kissed, he thought. A lonesome girl who liked him and who hadn't been kissed often.

For a moment she stood waiting; but he looked away. *Not that,* he thought. *I'm here under false pretenses. I've accepted her family's kindness knowing I'm going to hurt them all.* Moreover, he was holding a rifle in one hand and a fifteen-pound salmon in the other. Before he could think what to do with them she had moved away, saying she had to get back.

"Holland Gay is coming this afternoon," she said as Dave followed her toward the river.

They continued downstream on the river trail until

they came to a branch that took them back to the farm. Mrs. Covey met them at the kitchen door, brightening when she saw the salmon.

"Holland is partial to fish," she said.

Dave found Isaac Covey in the barn and consulted him about measuring off his claim. They drew a rough map on a board and covered it with figuring. Covey was full of advice.

"All you need to do now is pace off your boundaries approximate. Double-blaze trees or build monuments of rocks at the corners. Make the place a little too big. Before you prove up on it, you'll have to cut it down to size, but it's better to measure it off now with a few extry acres."

Dave borrowed an axe from Covey and spent the rest of the day picking and slashing his way through snarled forest, trying to lay out approximately straight boundaries. The fact that the river made an almost exact right-angle bend at one corner of his land greatly simplified his work, but the sun had set when he returned to the Covey place.

The family was just sitting down to supper with Holland Gay, who was a small, heavy, thirty-ish man with neatly combed black hair and restless blue eyes. He was wide rather than plump and had the high-pitched voice sometimes found in very muscular men. He paid no attention to the conversation at the table and interrupted it at intervals with unrelated bits of information, usually about himself.

"That jacket you see hangin' on that peg cost me twenty dollars," he said suddenly on one occasion. "Had to kill three fawns to get enough fawn-belly for it. There's a feller in Steilacoom he was a New York tailor. He made it for me to my fit. Charged me twenty dollars just for a jacket."

He looked from one to another as he spoke, but mostly at Ann. When he had finished, he lowered his head and became engrossed in his baked salmon. A moment later he let go with another burst, relevant to nothing.

"I run a saloon and never-at-any-time drink nothing stronger than buttermilk. I sell whisky to all who wants it and never-at-any-time drink none."

And so on throughout the meal. Dave decided that the man did not normally talk much but felt he had to talk now to make an impression on Ann and could do it only in volleys. And, being interested only in himself, he was stuck with himself as a subject.

After supper, Dave sat in the kitchen with the Coveys, giving Ann and Holland Gay the living room to themselves. In a little while Holland Gay came out and said he was leaving. Mrs. Covey looked startled.

"I thought you were going to stay the night," she said. "You can have Bobby's bed in the living room. He'll sleep on the floor."

"Got to get back," he said. "Business."

Isaac Covey got a lantern and gave it to Bobby telling him to go out and saddle Holland's horse. Mrs. Covey followed Holland to the back porch where they talked for a while in low tones.

Ann didn't bother to see her caller off; but as soon as he had gone, she came to the living room door and beckoned to Dave.

"Don't stay here tonight," she said when she had closed the door behind them. She spoke in an urgent whisper, her dark eyes dancing. "You've got to beat Holland to the land office!"

"You mean he's going to claim that land?"

"He is. He found a man who's agreed to file on it for him and live on it until he can sell his rights to the Fox Island place. Then this man will sign his rights to the river place over to Holland. Oh, he has it all schemed out. He was awful upset to find you on the place.

"He usually stays all night when he's here for supper. He meant to stay tonight but he changed his mind. He's going to get that man to file a claim in the morning—I know he is."

"Is there a land office in Steilacoom?"

"No. You'll have to go to Olympia. You go right past Steilacoom and nineteen miles farther. You take this road out of here to a fork about three miles down and take that—"

She gave him detailed directions and he remembered he had said he was lost.

"All right. I'm on my way. But tell me something, Ann. Why do you want me to have that place and Holland Gay not to have it?"

She looked at the floor and then at him, tipping her chin at him.

"I don't rightly know, David. I just do."

4

DAVE SLEPT three hours at the hotel at Steilacoom, then hit the road again and was at the land office in Olympia when it opened.

He pointed out his claim on a large map of Pierce County which the clerk unrolled—it was easy enough to locate because of the bend in the river. He told of the boundaries he had laid out and the clerk worked out a legal description of the property. Dave signed his name and it was done.

"You have to live on it five years, clear a reasonable amount of land and make other appreciable improvements," the clerk said in a routine voice. "Then you'll get title to it."

"Suppose somebody else files on that same land today. How will I be able to prove I filed first?"

The clerk looked at him sharply, but replied in the same bored tone. "Your claim has a number. Anybody who files later will have a higher number."

Dave walked the length of Olympia's winding, block-long business district, got breakfast at a log restaurant and started back to Steilacoom. Fog had rolled in from the Sound and smothered the road; he had an uneasy feeling that he traced back to the Naches pass and his sudden capture in the cloud bank. Occasionally he met travelers on horseback or in wagons; they materialized at close hand, nodded, and moved on into nothingness.

When he had passed the stockaded Hudson's Bay post a few miles south of Steilacoom, he suddenly met Holland Gay and another rider. They spoke and passed. A moment later Holland called to Dave and rode back alone.

"You son of a bitch, you filed on that claim!"

"If you want to talk to me," Dave said softly, "keep a civil tongue in your head."

Holland measured him. "Go ahead and build on it. Clear it. Put in your time and your work. You won't get it."

"If you want it so bad, buy my rights."

Holland was caught off guard. He took a moment to think this over, blinking like a fat little toad; then he was eager. "It ain't worth no cash, but it might cost me fifty dollars to get you off it; so I'll give you that. Fifty dollars will pay you for the time you wasted."

"It's worth five hundred. There's a meadow smack in the middle of those woods. Four acres all cleared for you." Dave added, "Ann showed it to me."

"That ain't so! If it is, I'll have it anyhow and I'll pay you no five hundred. I'll pay fifty, meadow or not, and no more."

"I'll see you in court," Dave said and kicked his horse forward. He half expected that Holland would call him back, but he did not.

Dave rode into Steilacoom from the south, passing a little water-powered lumber mill above some

Indian shacks on a creek that emptied into the bay. On an impulse, he stopped, found the owner, and asked him if he knew a man named Ben whose business took him around to different mills.

"I don't know," the mill owner, whose name was Chapman, said. "There was a fellow here a few months back who wanted to be my agent. He said he'd come around now and then to keep track of what lumber I had on hand and he'd send a ship to me when I had a surplus. He said he was already agent for three mills. He was a big gazabo. Black muttonchop whiskers."

"The man I'm looking for has light curly hair," Dave said. Bart Hadder might dye his hair and grow muttonchops, he thought.

"Don't sound like him."

"Did you take this fellow on?"

"Not much. I never have a surplus. Sell the stuff green as fast as I can cut it. . . . If I see that light-haired fellow, I'll tell him you're looking for him."

"That's all right," Dave said. "It isn't important."

He rode on into town, thinking it would be risky to question many people that way. Bart Hadder would hear that somebody was asking after him and would leave the Sound. It would be better to watch the Covey farm and wait. Sooner or later, Hadder would turn up for a spell of solitary drinking.

At the hotel he pulled off his boots and slept, not getting up when the landlady called him for lunch, and quickly dozing off again. Late in the afternoon a sharp knocking woke him. It was Sally Sugar.

"Well, I finally caught up with you," she said.

He was glad to see her, getting up to meet her in his stocking feet and leading her to a chair. She was an Indian, she wore moccasins and ate rattlesnake, she had been a white man's squaw, and yet she was a lady. Just naturally a lady, he thought, and you just naturally treated her like one.

"They won't take Indians at this hotel," she said, as if reading his thoughts. "I tried to get a room here night before last. Just now I told the landlady I'd come for your laundry."

"Where are you staying?"

"With an old Nisqually squaw in a shack at the mouth of the creek. It's kind of a fishy place, but she's clean for a Sound Indian. At least she isn't lousy."

"You haven't found your husband?"

"I've found out where he is—over near New York Alki in a new town they call Seattle. That's why I want to see you. I want to collect the new shawl and shoes you owe me. I want to be presentable. And I'll need five dollars more. That's the fare to Seattle by Murphy's Indian Canoe Express."

He gave her three gold eagles. She looked at him with a sudden soberness and for a moment he was afraid she wasn't satisfied; then she smiled her delicious smile and said, "It's been a long time since I've seen thirty dollars. This would buy me some material for a dress too, if I had time to make one."

"You look fine," he said. She wore the same wool skirt and beaded jacket she had worn on the trip, but they seemed spotless and unwrinkled.

Besides, she was a slender, full-breasted girl who could wrap herself in a wagon sheet and still look good to a man.

"Maybe I *should* stay here long enough to make a new dress," she said. "I do want to make a good impression on Roy."

He saw that under her chatter and her easy manner she was unsure of herself, feeling the humiliation of going to a husband who had once rejected her, yet seeing no choice. Without him, she was an Indian and must live with Indians. With him, her life could be to some extent that of a white woman—though she would be inviting another hurt. And there was something else, something more to it than this. Perhaps she loved him.

"Sally," Dave said, "you're a beautiful woman. If your husband doesn't beg you to come back to him, he's a thin-blooded dolt!"

"Well, thank you, Mr. Porter."

"Dave," he said.

"Dave."

"If he's stubborn, smile at him. You can make any man on earth jump through a hoop with that smile."

She gave him the smile. "I needed to hear those things. I needed them as much as I need a pair of shoes."

She got up and went to the door, then faced him. "Dave, I don't want to get you into trouble, but there's something I ought to tell you. Suchamuch is here."

"In Steilacoom?"

"He's living in Indiantown near me. I saw him on the pier on my way up here just now. He was with some other Indians and I think they were fishing."

Dave sat on the bed and began to pull on his boots. "I'll go right now."

"You'd better get the sheriff."

"He's sick." Dave got his hat and carbine. "Let's go."

They walked up Commercial Street, which climbed gently toward the outskirts of town. The fog had disappeared and a frail sun sparkled the bay. A salt breeze met them at the top of the rise and molded Sally's skirt against her legs. They could see Indiantown ahead of them, shacks strung along the shore and clustered at the mouth of the creek below the mill Dave had visited that morning. Just below them, this side of the first shacks, a pier stretched into the bay, a loading place for the mill. Three Indians were there, two fishing, the other lying on his back with his feet hanging over the water and a black hat over his face.

"That's Suchamuch," Sally said. "The one who's asleep. The other two are Nisquallies."

"You wait here," Dave said when they reached the shore end of the pier.

"No sir! Maybe I can save your life again—and earn another thirty dollars."

The Indians who were fishing gave them brief glances as they approached. They had caught several flounder, which lay on the dock beside a quart bottle of whisky, nearly empty. Suchamuch slept with one arm flung straight out from his shoulder. The ivory handle of Dave's Colt protruded from his belt.

Dave seized the revolver and yanked it free. Suchamuch spun over on his stomach and looked up stupidly. He got to his feet. Dave cocked the carbine and covered him with it, handing the pistol to Sally.

The other two Indians shifted their positions so they could watch what was going on, but neither took his line from the water. Sally said something to them in Chinook.

"Start walking," Dave said to Suchamuch. "All the way to the fort. To Captain Maloney."

"Dirty Boston," Suchamuch grunted. He didn't budge.

"Move!"

Suchamuch glanced at the muzzle of the carbine and seemed to reach a decision. He spat at Dave's feet, tossed his head, and stood with his hands on his hips.

I won't shoot him in cold blood and he knows it, Dave thought. *He can stand there glaring all day and I won't shoot him.*

Boots sounded hollowly on the pier as men came to watch. Half a dozen, white and Indian, had already crowded up. Others were running along the shore toward the pier.

Dave handed the carbine to Sally. He seized the Indian's wrist, trying for an arm lock, but he had to spin away to avoid Suchamuch's knee. For an instant they faced each other, then Suchamuch attacked, aiming kicks at Dave's groin with first one foot and then the other, moving like a goose-stepping toy soldier, but with remarkable speed.

Dave backed away, dodging, protecting himself ungracefully with his hands. Foot-fighting was new to him, but he solved it instinctively. Dodging one kick, he spun completely around and outside the next, caught the foot, lifted it, and gave the ankle a wrench that sent the Indian sprawling.

Before Dave could take his advantage, Suchamuch was on his feet again and charging, this time with his head down. He aimed at Dave's midsection, then brought his ugly, flattened head up like a bull, narrowly missing Dave's jaw. Dave faded back with the charge and spun away, barely keeping his feet, but he was ready for the next charge. Holding his fists in front of his chin, he stood his ground and brought them down in two rapid rabbit punches that dropped Suchamuch unconscious on the dock.

A cheer went up from the crowd, which was large now and still growing. Dave was startled to see Holland Gay in the front row, staring placidly. A little fat man pushed up and touched the felled Suchamuch with the toe of his foot. It was the deputy sheriff.

"Don't you know better'n to pick a fight with a Injun?" he said to Dave. "It makes trouble."

"That's Suchamuch," somebody in the crowd said. "He's a bad one, Sheriff."

Sally had bent over Suchamuch and he stirred. She came up with Dave's purse, looking into it. She was still clutching Dave's guns. "There's only about twenty dollars here."

"What you doin'? Robbin' him?" The deputy demanded. "I'll take that purse!"

Sally avoided him and Dave took the money and guns.

"I said I'd take that purse. Them guns too."

The crowd booed and the deputy hesitated. Dave slipped the purse into a pocket and shoved the revolver under his belt across his stomach.

"What was the trouble?" The deputy asked, sensing that the crowd was with Dave. He asked it of the nearest bystander, who was Holland Gay.

"I know this feller," Holland said, nodding at Dave. "He's a troublemaker. He jumped a claim up on the Puyallup."

Suchamuch got to his feet, sick and reeling, shaking his head violently. The crowd shuffled back. He seemed to have trouble seeing clearly but finally fastened his eyes on Dave.

"I kill you, Boston. I kill you some day."

He staggered over to the whisky bottle, sat down on the dock and drank. The two Nisquallies were still fishing.

"If you want to make yourself useful," Dave said to the deputy, "take him up to the fort. Captain Maloney will be glad to see him."

He took Sally's arm and led her through the crowd. Somebody slapped him on the back.

They went into town and into Balch's where Sally bought her shawl and shoes. She left him there, although he protested.

"Come to the hotel," he said. "They'll give you a room or I'll tear the place down."

"Aren't you the hell-roarer though! Just because you licked Suchamuch . . . No, Dave, I'll go and have boiled fish with my Nisqually squaw. Look me up if you get to Seattle—they say it's at the head of a bay east of New York Alki. My married name is Smallwood—Mrs. Roy Smallwood."

Dave spent the night in town, visiting a saloon after supper and finding himself something of a celebrity. In the morning he drew the rest of his money from Balch and bought the tools he would need to build a cabin. He rented an extra horse and a packsaddle at the livery and made the trip to his claim.

Ann came onto the porch as he reached Covey's and he waved, not intending to stop; but she called and came running across the clearing to him.

"Holland beat you, David! He came last night with another man and supplies and he knew about the meadow and made me show it to him! The man put up a tent and has got some Indians to help him and is building a cabin. They beat you!"

5

THE INDIAN CANOE which took Sally the thirty-three miles to Seattle had been burned and hacked out of a forty-foot cedar log. It had been painted a streaked red and protected against seagoing *tamanohuses* by rows of shells along the gunwales. It was paddled by ten Klalam Indians and navigated by a grim Irishman who sat in the stern and barked orders in Chinook.

Sally was the only passenger, sitting amidships on an inverted bucket cushioned with a blanket. It was an uncomfortable arrangement but she forgot her numbness in the restful beauty of fir-topped bluffs, sandy beaches, timbered islands. The Indians chanted as they paddled, repeating the same theme with constant variations. And though the Klalam words were strange to her, she found herself saying them too, softly, and found a meaning in them. When the breeze was favorable, they put up a square sail woven of reeds, and the chanting and paddling gave way to chatter and pipe-smoking. She had a curious thought that perhaps the moment of death was eternal, and she almost wished she could fall dead now. For what better heaven could there be than to cruise forever in the sunshine with a breeze ruffling your hair and happy people around you?

They beached at a sandspit for a lunch of smoked

salmon and an hour's rest, then set off again, reaching New York Alki in the late afternoon. "Alki" was a Chinook word meaning "after while." New York After While. Well, it was a hopeful name, Sally thought—more hopeful than the scattering of cabins on the picturesque point seemed to warrant. After exchanging mail they paddled on to the head of the bay and the settlement called Seattle.

Sally left the canoe on a beach beside a big dock. On the shore above, men were busy around a screaming, steam-powered saw. Oxen were skidding a big log down to the mill from the higher ground behind it. Beyond the skid road, she found a newly staked out town with some of the streets scarcely discernible. There were not more than a dozen finished houses and cabins (not counting Indian shacks along the beach), and two or three more being built.

At one of these a woman wielded a hammer, helping put on the sheathing, and Sally asked her if she knew where Roy Smallwood lived. She looked at Sally in surprise, as white people always did when they heard her English, and pointed to a two-story house at the very edge of the logged-off area with the wall of the forest behind it. It was a fine house with a big porch and real glass windows, although it was unpainted. . . . Red would be a nice color, Sally thought—red with white trim, like that hotel in Steilacoom.

No one answered her knock, though she thought she heard a voice from inside. She peeked through one of the porch windows and then went in, entering a scantily furnished living room. She called "Hello!" There was a sound from the back of the house, a sound like a snore. After a moment, she went back.

Roy Smallwood lay prone on the kitchen table in the midst of disorder. A fat squaw lay on the floor in front of the stove, snoring. A chair had been overturned, one of its rungs broken. There was a gallon jug under the table. The room reeked of alcohol.

"Who is it?" Roy said, without moving.

Sally didn't answer. She stood in the doorway, stunned, angry, hurt—and glad. The scene she had dreaded wouldn't take place tonight; perhaps it never would take place. There was no need to ask him to take her back. He needed her and she was back.

She went over and kicked the squaw, not gently.

"*Klatawa!*" she said. "Get out!"

The woman looked up with eyes that were dull black beads. Sally kicked her again. She got up awkwardly, muttering.

"Outside!" Sally hissed, pointing to the back door.

The woman collected herself for an argument. She began to speak angrily in a language Sally didn't understand. Sally got a stick of kindling wood and hit her across the stomach. The squaw made a half-hearted stand at the door, but Sally pushed her out, took the stick to her backside and ran her clear out of the yard.

Back in the kitchen, she found Roy had got off the table and was staring at her unbelievingly.

"Sally! Sally Sugar! Is it really you?"

"So you went back to this!" she said. "There were times when I wished you bad luck, Roy—but not this! I thought you had it whipped. I underestimated myself, Roy. I helped you whip it. I kept you straight. I was the only thing that did."

"Sally Sugar!" Nothing she had said reached him. He tried to focus bloodshot eyes. He seemed an old man, though he was barely thirty. His sandy hair had faded and thinned. The snub-nosed face that she remembered as frank and boyish was lined and bloated.

He got the jug from under the table and poured himself half a tumbler of whisky, shaking badly and spilling some of it. He raised the glass with an attempt at jauntiness. Sally knocked it out of his hand.

He stood up, outraged, and swung wildly at her. She pushed him toward his chair, but he missed it and crashed to the floor. She left him there and started a fire in the stove, got water from a well in the yard, put a kettle of coffee on.

She found a cloth and bent over him to bathe his face. Seeing that he was filthy, she took off his clothes and gave him a bath then and there. He had very little fight left in him. She made him drink coffee until he was sick, then led him upstairs and put him to bed.

"Sally," he said pathetically, his voice thick and far away. "Get me sober."

"I'm going to."

"Didn't think I'd make it this time. Couldn't—bear—the thought—of sobering up."

"You'll make it, Roy."

"Don't leave me," he said.

She sat beside him until he fell asleep; then she searched the house for whisky, threw out all she could find, and began to tidy up the house.

In a way, she was happy. There was something flattering about Roy's drunkenness, if you wanted to see it that way. He'd been a heavy drinker when she first knew him, but this had seemed to stem from the loneliness of a soldier at a remote outpost. At least, he had quit entirely soon after marrying her. Now, without her, he'd gone back to the bottle. Could it be he was lonely again? . . . But her happiness was selfish, she thought, and would be short-lived unless she could help him. It wasn't going to be easy to get him straightened out without the exacting demands of a military life to back her up.

She was cleaning the kitchen when a knock called her to the front door. It was a big bear of a man with black muttonchop whiskers.

He grinned at her familiarly and said, to himself rather than her, "Well, look at this!" Then he began to speak in halting Chinook.

"I probably speak better English than you do," Sally said. "What do you want?"

He laughed. He had a round, cheerful face and very white teeth. "I came to see Roy Smallwood. I'm beginning to hope he isn't in."

"He's sick," Sally said curtly. "I'm his wife."

"Well, fancy that!" he said, sounding as if he didn't believe her.

"Is there anything I can do?"

The big man lowered his voice to a confidential tone. "Is he drunk?"

"He's sick. He's asleep now and can't see you."

"I'm agent for his mill. I have a ship that wants some cedar for San Francisco. Do you know if he has any cut?"

"He owns a mill?" Sally said.

"You didn't know that?"

"Not that big mill down by the dock?"

"No, not that one. His is down the shore a way. You say you're his wife?"

"I just got here today," Sally said, vaguely embarrassed. "We've been separated for a long time."

The big man lowered his voice again and said, his eyes twinkling, "Why don't you ask me in? I'll tell you about his mill."

"I'd rather hear about it from Roy." She started to close the door.

"How about that cedar?"

"Can you come tomorrow? Roy won't be well enough to see you, but I can ask him about the cedar and tell you."

The big man sighed. "All right, I'll come tomorrow."

"I'll tell him you were here."

"Weller is the name, ma'am," he said with a jaunty little bow. "Ben Weller."

6

WHEN DAVE REACHED the meadow, leading his horses through the tangled woods, he found the first logs of a cabin laid in just about the place where he had thought he would build. Beside them a small man in a red undershirt was notching a log with a double-bitted axe. A little way off, two Indians swung axes at a fir. An ox team stood by.

The claim jumper stuck his axe in the log when he saw Dave and picked up a long, over-and-under rifle. He was middle-aged, wiry, shrewd-faced. Dave recognized him as the companion of Holland Gay on the road to Olympia.

Dave had a way of turning calm when he was angry. His expression grew pleasant, his voice became a purr, and yet there was an iciness to his manner more foreboding than vehemence. He greeted the man politely, introducing himself. In return, the claim jumper said his name was Pete Nippin. They didn't shake hands.

"I guess you know I filed on this ground," Dave said.

"Hell, I filed too." He was chewing tobacco and spoke unplainly.

"How much is Holland Gay paying you?-'

Except for a smug grin, Nippin ignored the question. "You fixin' to build on it?"

"I'm going to start right now."

"Well, I'll outstay you. I'm the meanest little sack of fishhooks you ever saw."

"No," Dave said. "You won't outstay me."

He rode to the other side of the meadow, to a place where the ground rose and dipped. He'd build a cabin on the high ground, he thought, and dig a well on the low. He turned the horses to graze and began to unpack his outfit, thinking in a detached way what a strange country this was, this great forest and inland sea which just a scattering of white men had found. There was more than enough for all who would work; but along with the industrious ones were the shiftless and the sharp and the violent, attracted to a land where boundaries weren't precise and law officers were few. There weren't many of these parasites, but they could spoil it for the rest.

He was jolted out of his thoughts by the crack of a rifle across the meadow and a bullet smashed into a wooden bucket he had bought that morning in Steilacoom. He dived for his carbine and lay flat.

He could see no one except the two Indians, who had stopped work and were staring toward him. In a moment another shot hit the bucket, coming from behind the knee-high wall of Nippin's cabin a hundred yards away; then another. The man was shooting at the bucket and nothing else.

Dave got up and crossed the meadow. Nippin rose from behind his breastworks, grinning.

"Want to show you I hit what I aim at," he said, his finger on the trigger of his double-barreled rifle. "And I might as well tell you I reload a barr'l before

I fire t'other. Don't get no ideas about catchin' me with a empty gun."

"You owe me a bucket."

"Boy, you know you ain't goin' to get no bucket out of me."

"Put down your gun and I'll take it out of your hide."

"No thank you sir. I *dee*cline. You got fifteen years on me and thirty pounds."

"I'll say it as clearly as I can, Nippin. Get off this land. If you don't intend to, you better aim your next shot at me. Do you understand that?"

Nippin grinned in his sarcastic way. "Well now, boy, I might do that."

Dave turned abruptly and walked to his side of the meadow. He had an uneasy feeling about getting a bullet in the back. It hardly seemed likely that a man would kill for land that would not be his own, but Nippin seemed on the simple side—you couldn't tell what he'd do. Dave flinched when another shot crashed into what was left of the bucket.

He had little appetite for a fight over the place, though he didn't see how else he could deal with Nippin. He considered packing up and taking another claim, but quickly decided against it. There was plenty of available land all around here but surely none with a meadow that would give it cash value. There was no telling how long it would take him to find Bart Hadder and he was going to need that cash.

He picked up his shovel from among his belongings and went to the low ground, intending to dig a well before he did anything else. Nippin changed his target then and began to blast away at a fir seedling ten feet away from where Dave was working. Dave pretended to pay no attention, but it was nerve-racking to work with bullets whistling that close.

When he was three feet down, he paused to rest. Across the meadow, Nippin sat on a log, loading his gun. His axe was stuck in the end of the same log, its handle a white line against the forest. The axe gave Dave an idea.

He got his carbine, knelt in the hole he had dug, and aimed. Even with a full-length rifle, it would have been an odds-on shot; with the carbine it was a wild chance. But he had that rare, inexplicable confidence known to dice players and marksmen, the feeling that he couldn't miss.

He fired and hit. The axe handle vibrated like a piece of watch spring and the axe toppled out of the log. Nippin looked from the axe to Dave in amazement. He did no more shooting that day.

Ann and her father came into the clearing. Covey stopped to talk to Nippin. Ann hurried on to where Dave was digging.

"We heard shooting!" Her excitement shone in her eyes, giving her a radiance that was almost palpable. Dave had the thought that he would have felt her presence even if he hadn't seen or heard her.

"My neighbor and I were having target practice," he said, leaning on his shovel and grinning. "I think I won the prize."

"You weren't shooting at each other?"

"Not exactly."

She glanced toward Nippin. "I think it's awful of Holland to do this! And I'm mad at Father for letting that man use our oxen. David, why don't you run that man off right now?"

"Somebody would get killed."

"There must be some way," she said, then suddenly changed the subject, asking him about his plans for building, chattering about wells and cabins, crops and livestock. Isaac Covey joined them, making it a point to shake hands with Dave.

"Whichever of you wins out, I get a neighbor," he said, grinning and then growing serious. "I felt I had to loan them oxen when Holland asked me. But you can use them, too, when Nippin is done with them."

"Father," Ann said. "Ask Dave to dinner."

"We told Hannah we was going to bring you—if you wasn't perforated," Covey said.

As it turned out, Dave not only went back with them for the noon meal but took most of his meals there for the next several days and slept in their barn, in the bunk Bart Hadder had built, until the roof was on his cabin. At times he called himself a hypocrite, but there was no help for it. Finding his man meant being friendly with the Coveys, accepting their hospitality while he kept his ears open for news of Uncle Ben.

When he found he could do Isaac Covey a favor, he jumped at the chance—even though it meant parting with money he didn't have to spare. Covey had a chance to buy a dozen shoats from a farmer who was leaving for the California gold fields. The price was twenty-five dollars for the lot, which was cheap for that country at that time. The pigs could root for themselves on the Covey place and in the fall would be worth four or five times that much. Covey didn't have the money and one rainy evening when he and Dave were alone in the living room he haltingly asked if Dave had it to spare. Dave gave it to him at once, delighting him and putting him in a talkative mood.

"I'll pay you back in the fall with good interest," he said. "Ten per cent a month."

"Forget the interest," Dave said, hoping he would be two thousand miles away by fall and thinking he'd never see the money again. "I've already had the interest. I've eaten it."

"Well, it's kindly of you to make the loan. I asked Holland for the money but he said no. Said a b'ar might get the pigs, or a pant'er. Besides, I already owe him a considerable bit."

Covey went on to talk about his affairs then, making clear what Dave already suspected—his interest to Holland Gay as a son-in-law was largely mercenary.

"You know," he said, "I even got my crops mortgaged—along with my rights to the claim and every animal I own. What cash I get from the wheat and potatoes will go as soon as I get it. And the worst of it is everything else comes due this fall."

"Who holds the mortgage on your claim?"

"Holland does, and on the horse and oxen too. He'll give me more time, I guess—if Ann don't get sassy and make him hostyle. I wish the girl would make up her mind, but I won't pressure her the way Hannah does."

Dave grinned. "He's hardly what a young girl dreams about."

"Well, he's what they dream about, you might say, when they get the silliness out of them and get a houseful of kids and no money to buy shoes. He can provide. I can't say I warm up to the man the way I might to another, but I believe he'd give Ann a good life."

Under the deep tan of Covey's face there was a pallor that gave it a grayish cast. The man looked tired, worked out. Dave thought: *How old and tired do you have to be to talk like that? How much drudgery and defeat do you have to know to start believing what it's convenient to believe?* Then he saw Covey studying him, waiting for his reaction, and he saw there was a sly side to this talk. He said, "As a saloonkeeper's wife?"

"He'll sell the saloon. He's got other irons in the fire."

"I know."

"Well, it will take a smart man and a stubborn one to keep him from takin' that claim. You got money to fall back on?"

"Precious little," Dave said. He was about to add that it was going fast, but—having just handed Covey some of it—caught himself.

"Got any debts?"

"No."

"That's a great advantage. You ought to make out fine on that place, if you get it. That meadow is a lucky thing. 'Course a farmer needs a wife. There's twice as many men as women in this country and a good girl is hard to find. 'Course, when the wagons start to roll in, it will be better all around. People, that's what this country needs . . ." And he lapsed into his discourse on the benefits the Naches road would bring.

Dave half listened, realizing that he as well as Holland Gay was under consideration as a possible son-in-law. It was not a thought to please a young man who had always liked his freedom; and since he was not the home-seeking settler Covey thought him, he felt particularly uncomfortable. Still, he could wish that circumstances were different. Ann was a fine girl and a man had to settle down sometime.

On the morning of his second day on the claim, Dave looked up from his well-digging and saw three Puyallups staring somberly down at him. One of them spoke in Chinook, finally making Dave understand that they would work five days for a shirt apiece. It was a great bargain—especially since dry goods, unlike food, were cheap enough in Steilacoom. The men worked well and in a matter of days the cabin was up, the roof tight, a fireplace built of stones from the river, crude furniture knocked together, and a trail cut from Dave's side of the meadow to the riverbank.

One of the Indians, a boy about twenty named Tilluk, grew especially friendly. He stayed on the claim when Dave was away, brought salmon and berries, and took it upon himself to instruct Dave in Chinook. In the evenings at Covey's, Dave studied the vocabulary Captain Maloney had given him, sometimes going over it with Ann, and the next day he would try out the words on Tilluk. It was a primitive language without tenses or conjugations and, except for a bit of difficulty in pronunciation, he could soon speak it almost as well as the Puyallups.

Nippin made himself as annoying a neighbor as possible. After he got over the shock of Dave's lucky shot, he again took to shooting at anything across the meadow that caught his fancy. Half of Dave's equipment was hit and one side of his cabin was pockmarked with bullet holes, though Nippin never fired at it when anyone was inside.

He had other tricks too. When Dave was shoring up the sides of his well after hitting water at fifteen feet, a grass snake came down on top of him, writhing and hissing. It was harmless but it gave him a bad moment. He tossed it out and climbed up the ladder in time to see Nippin scurry into the woods, giggling childishly.

Another time, Nippin gave Dave's Indians a quart of whisky, and two of them were soon unfit for work. However, this prank backfired, more or less literally, when he put a bullet through a hat one of them had left on a log. The drunken Indian snatched up Dave's carbine and returned a shot at Nippin's hat, which was on his head. He missed, but not by much.

Whenever Dave faced the man he found himself confronted by the double-barreled rifle. If there was to be a fight over the claim, it apparently would have to be a gunfight. Well, there was no hurry about getting the man off, he decided. He'd wait till Bart Hadder was safe in Captain Maloney's guardhouse and he was ready to sell his rights and go back to Illinois.

At Covey's he occasionally tried to lead the conversation around to Uncle Ben, but without much success. Although they had spoken freely of him at first, the family now never mentioned him. When Dave quietly questioned Bobby or the two little girls about their uncle, he was met with such reticence that he wondered if they had been instructed to avoid the subject. Ann had become strangely suspicious of him that day she had shown him the meadow and it seemed to him that she must have mentioned her suspicion to the others.

When his cabin was finished, he took to visiting Steilacoom two or three nights a week, looking over the stores, the saloons, the card games. Occasionally he asked a casual question about a man named Ben something-or-other who traveled around to lumber mills. On one occasion he heard again of a dark man with muttonchop whiskers who was agent for some of the smaller mills. His informant was uncertain just which mills, but he thought the DeLin mill on Commencement Bay might be one of them.

This was at the mouth of the Puyallup only about ten miles from Steilacoom, and Dave rode there next morning. He found a fine natural harbor between timbered points with great tide flats at its head. Indian canoes slid over the rippled water, trolling for salmon. Here and there, Indian shacks dotted the shore. A thinly wooded spot near the mouth of the river was a cemetery, its trees adorned with the wrapped corpses of hundreds of Puyallups. A sailing ship was anchored off the mill, which was on a creek at the mouth of a wooded gulch. Half a dozen Indians stood around the saw, having come for miles to stare in fascination at the strange machinery.

DeLin, the owner, turned out to be a bull-chested young man with a heavy Swedish accent.

"You're looking for Ben Veller maybe," he said when Dave had asked his question.

"Veller?"

"No," DeLin said. "Veller. Vith a 'w.' He is agent for me but he don't come around often. See t'at ship? She's taking t'ree hundred fifty t'ousand feet from me. She's been anchored nine veeks and she ain't half loaded yet. My saw is so slow I don't often have no lumber extra for the agent to sell. I t'ink he qvit me."

"Where can I find him?"

DeLin scratched his head. "I never could find the scallyvag myself ven I vanted him. Say, vy are you looking for him? He cheat you at cards? He cheated me, I t'ink."

"That's the man," Dave said.

"You know vat I t'ink? He don't make much money from lumber. T'at agent talk is to cover up for monkey-business."

DeLin had no idea what town Weller's base might be in or what other mills he represented. But at least Dave felt he could now be sure the muttonchopped

Weller and Bart Hadder were the same man. He had changed his appearance and he seemed to have made a point of keeping his headquarters a secret. He was jumpy. Finding him was going to be a touchy business, and taking him touchier. Still, there was satisfaction in knowing that even in this remote country Bart Hadder was living in uncertainty and fear.

7

CAPTAIN GEORGE B. MCCLELLAND surveyed the Naches pass for the Army. He decided that a road was out of the question—"impossible" was the word he used in his report. The Army abandoned the project.

When this news reached Steilacoom, the countryside hummed with indignation. To men and women who had come two thousand miles by ox team and hacked homesteads out of the overwhelming forest, nothing was "impossible"; and their dream was not to be exploded by a captain fresh from Texas who had been appalled by the sight of real mountains. They did what they had always done when bad luck hit. They got together and encouraged one another and cursed and laughed and found hope in their own strength. And put another paragraph in the history books.

Dave rode to the Steilacoom meeting in the Covey wagon, sitting in the back with Ann and the children. It was a warm July evening and the meeting was on a hillside north of town. Most of the farmers from this part of the Sound were there, along with most of the population of Olympia and all that of Steilacoom, including children, dogs and Indians. Even so, the crowd was not a large one—two hundred people maybe—and the Coveys and others sat in their wagons in easy range of the speakers' voices. Ann and Dave wandered off and stood with the crowd gathered around a cedar stump from which Lafayette Balch made the first speech.

"Everybody who has a stake in this country knows we have to have that road," he said. "Maybe if we petition Congress and sit back and wait a few years, we'll get it. But we can't afford to wait. Right now wagon trains are on their way across the country. Some of them would come here if there was a way in. We want that road now and there's only one way we'll get in. We'll build it ourselves!"

There was a great silence and then a great cheer. The dream was whole again. They'd build the consarned road themselves.

"We'll organize a work party," Balch went on. "We'll start from this end. Whitfield Kirtley is here tonight from east of the mountains. He's going back and organize another party among the settlers over there. They'll start from that end.

"Anybody who's been over that trail knows it isn't going to be easy. A few of us can't do it. It will mean work from every man here, and money too. We'll have to lend our tools and our animals. We'll have a big work party to feed and we'll have to give part of our crops. I'll donate supplies for the first two weeks, but that isn't even a beginning."

He went on to give the details of the plan he and some others had worked out. In addition to the party of volunteer workers, they would hire Indians, paying them in dry goods that Balch would furnish at cost. A young engineer named Allen would be in charge of the western work party. A man named Burge would be responsible for the supply train. Captain Maloney, as disappointed by the Army decision as the settlers, had agreed to lend horses.

Dr. William Tolmie, Hudson's Bay factor at Fort Nisqually, climbed up on the stump beside Balch and made a little speech wishing luck to the project. The Hudson's Bay Company and its subsidiary, the Puget Sound Agricultural Company, had always opposed any measure that would encourage immigration, preferring to keep the country as much to themselves as possible. Everyone there knew that and Tolmie admitted it frankly. "But," he concluded, speaking with an Edinburgh accent, "it's a hopeless policy. If your own army can't discourage you Americans, the Company can't. So, as a token of our good wishes, we'll contribute a hundred dollars and enough blankets to pay twenty Indians for a week's work."

Balch spoke again, saying that someone had suggested they hold a dance to raise funds and to give the work party a send-off. He thought it was a good idea.

This news excited Ann. "David, I want to go! I've only been to one dance in my life."

He stood staring at nothing over the heads of the crowd, wanting to ask her to go with him and telling himself he couldn't. It had been a long time since he had taken a girl to a dance—the last time had been when Paul, his brother, was alive. But he couldn't start that now. He'd mess things up for Ann and maybe for himself too. And then he saw Holland

Gay in the crowd ahead of them, looking up at Balch and blinking stupidly.

And then he had asked her and she was saying she'd love to and moving possessively close with her arm soft and warm against his. It had been a long time since he had known even this intimacy and it stirred him. He slipped his hand across her slender back and around her waist, thinking what a handsome girl she was, thinking that he had to have her, and then getting hold of himself and moving away. He excused himself and went over to speak to a man he was acquainted with, though he hardly knew what to say to him. In a little while, Holland Gay saw Ann and went to her; and though it grated upon him, Dave left them alone.

He and Ann rode home in silence that night, sitting in the wagon bed with little Alice asleep against his shoulder and Ella in Ann's arms. He was restless, dissatisfied with himself, impatient of the long ride home. Two or three times he caught Ann studying him as if he puzzled her. Well, no doubt he did. And he cursed himself—both for walking away from her so abruptly and for not having walked away sooner.

The next afternoon Holland Gay came into the meadow, stopping a moment at Nippin's cabin before crossing to Dave's. Dave, who was working with Tilluk on a lean-to for his horse, greeted him cheerfully.

"Hello, Holland. Decide to buy me out?"

Holland ignored the question and turned to look

over the meadow. "If I'd known this here was here, I'd had this place long ago. You know why there ain't no trees here? An Injun camp was here. Many years ago in the past. That's what it was, an Injun camp."

He went over and looked in Dave's well and spat in it.

"You do that again," Dave said, "and you'll go in after it."

"On my property I do as I please," Holland said, his voice a righteous whine. He came over and faced Dave. "You think you can cheat me outen my property. Go ahead and try. Business is business. And there is some things that ain't business. Like Ann. I give you fair warnin'. Don't take her to that dance."

"All right—if she tells me she doesn't want to go."

"She's a kindly girl and won't do that. I'm a hard man and a fair man. I give you fair warnin'."

Dave felt anger rise in him with a violence that he seldom knew. He had to make an effort to keep his voice down. "She's your property too. Is that it?"

Holland paid no attention to the question. He was interested only in what he himself had to say.

"I know what you are. I seen you beat that poor Injun and rob him while that squaw held a gun on him." He repeated this accusation in Chinook for the benefit of Tilluk.

Dave made no reply, seeing Holland clearly for the first time, seeing he was capable of any meanness and capable of believing himself a fine man while he did it. To him the truth was not what he saw or heard but any distortion that would make himself seem right. It was no use trying to reach him, for he could have no belief in anything but such distortions. Holland Gay didn't live in the same world with normal people.

Dave turned back to his work. Holland crossed to Nippin's and after a few minutes left the meadow. Tilluk watched him go.

"I know that man," Tilluk said. "His heart is black. He lied when he spoke to me. I have heard how you were robbed in the mountains by Tsitsiemuth, who is called Suchamuch by Bostons and whose heart is black. I have heard how you fought him and took what was yours."

Dave was amazed that a sympathetic account of his fight should have got so far into the woods, and he was pleased.

"You know the man who was here?"

"He is called Holland Gay and he is a bad man. He sells whisky to Indians." Unlike Dave's other two helpers, Tilluk had no use for whisky.

"Are you sure of that, Tilluk?"

"On Fox Island he has a machine to make whisky and he sells it to Indians."

The dance was held in an empty warehouse near the pier where Dave had fought Suchamuch. There were two fiddlers and, since it was a pleasant night, one of them played on the doorstep and some of the couples formed squares on the pier.

There was a good deal of unscheduled excitement. One of the Chapman girls danced right off the pier and nearly drowned. Somebody spiked the punch and Grandma Pinker got tipsy and delivered a temperance lecture. There was a dog fight in the middle of the dance floor. Zola Beech lost her petticoat.

In spite of having been to only one other dance, Ann was grace itself, floating on the music, becoming part of it, and onlookers picked her out to watch. Dave was proud of her and at the same time irked by the thought of folks calling them a nice couple, which they no doubt were doing. When Holland Gay began claiming Ann for every other dance, he made no objection.

After a little of this, however, Ann gave Holland an abrupt refusal, turning away from him when he tried to lead her out on the floor.

"I'm sorry, Holland, but I'm going to dance all the rest with David."

When Dave took her out on the pier during an intermission she said, "I hope I never have to dance with Holland again."

"That's no way to talk about your future husband."

Ann gave him a haughty look. "It's just that he's an awful dancer," she said quickly.

They walked the length of the pier, which culminated in a large dock. Other couples were here, standing close together, gazing at the dark islands beyong the starlit tide rips.

Ann knew many of the people at the dance and she

had been pointing out acquaintances to Dave all evening. So at first he paid little attention when she looked back toward the warehouse and said, "Oh, that looks like—" and broke off, throwing Dave a quick glance. But when she immediately pointed across the water and began ticking off the names of the islands, he wondered if she was trying to divert his attention and he looked back.

"There's who?" he asked.

"Nobody. I made a mistake . . . That's Fox Island on the right."

A group of men were standing around a dice game toward the shore end of the pier. Their faces were dim in the lantern light, but he could make out some that he knew. If the big, dark man hadn't left the group just then, Dave wouldn't have noticed him; but he walked to the warehouse and stood in the doorway for an idle look inside. There was something familiar about the way he moved and, seeing him silhouetted in the doorway, Dave tensed.

"David, look," Ann was saying. "Next is McNeil Island . . ."

He muttered something and left her, striding along the pier, remembering the trial of the well-dressed man who swaggered into the courtroom as the man in the doorway now swaggered on into the building. Dave dodged around strollers, passed Holland Gay talking to two men who towered over him. He reached the doorway and could see his man inside, walking the length of the warehouse toward the door in the other end. He followed, slowing and trying to appear casual when the big man paused and glanced back before stepping into the darkness. He had a clear view of the round, insolent face and he was sure now. This was Bart Hadder.

Dave had left his revolver under some potato sacks in the Covey wagon, which was tied with some others on the other side of the road, and he went to get it. Hadder was walking up the road toward the center of town. Dave heard rapid footsteps behind him and turned to see two men hurrying along the side of the warehouse. They crossed the road behind him, and one of them called to him.

"Hey, Porter!"

Dave turned and waved, not recognizing them, and kept walking toward the wagons. They broke into a run and came up with him as he neared the first wagon.

"I'm in a hell of a hurry," he said. "What do you want?"

"You David Porter?"

"Yes."

A fist hit him on the side of the head and sent him reeling. Another caught him from the other side. He threw up his hands to protect his head and took a solid punch in the stomach. He was on the ground, sick and dizzy, thinking that he must get up. The men stood waiting, grinning at him. He got to his knees and tried to pick out the Covey wagon, making a wild plan to dash for it and get the revolver, but he didn't even have strength to get to his feet.

One of the men helped him up and the other hit

him over the eye with a roundhouse right. Somebody was pushing his face into the dirt. He took a kick in the ribs that felt like a sword thrust, and then he was unconscious.

He came back slowly, drifting through a weird world of hands and voices until a stab of pain brought body and mind together. He was on a sofa in somebody's home. The room was full of people. His chest was tightly bandaged. A man was doing something to his forehead and speaking softly.

"Just two or three more stitches and I'll be done. Just lie quiet."

"Has he come to?" Ann's voice said.

He winced as the needle and gut went through the flesh over his eye and his slight motion brought a pressure in his chest that made him gasp.

"You've got a busted rib, son. Just lie quiet. I'm Dr. Spinning—doctor and blacksmith."

The nightmare of his beating came back to him vaguely and was real only because of his pain and weakness. What he remembered clearly was Bart Hadder swaggering up the road toward town.

"I've got to get out of here," he said. He tried to get up but was overwhelmed by pain and nausea.

"Lie down!" Dr. Spinning said sharply.

He took another stitch in the cut over Dave's eye. Dave lay back, trying to think. Hadder would be in a card game somewhere. Or back at the dance. Or in bed at the hotel. Or on his way to Covey's for a bender.

He gathered his strength and stood up, pushing the doctor aside.

"David, you lie down!" Ann said, trying to lead him back to the sofa.

He staggered to the door, discovering that Holland Gay was among the others in the room. He saw the wagon in front of the house, got to it, and got his gunbelt from under the seat. While he was fumbling with the buckle, Dr. Spinning and Ann came up to him.

"David, take off that gun!" Ann said.

"Listen to me," Spinning said. "You're sick and you're in shock. You can't think clearly. the fight's over. If you kill one of those men now, you're guilty of murder."

"Doctor, can Ann stay at your house for an hour or so?" Dave said. "I'm going to take the wagon. Don't worry—I'm not going after the men who beat me up."

They let him go then, and he drove to the hotel. No one named Weller was staying there. He visited the saloons, finding only one card game going and his man not there. He went back to the dance, to Indiantown, to the saloons again, and saw nothing of Bart Hadder. It never occurred to him to visit the ship that was anchored a little way off Balch's pier.

Twice during his search, the pressing pain in his chest became unbearable and he was stricken with nausea and dizziness. By the time he got back to Spinning's, he was so weak and ill that he didn't see how he was going to get down from the seat. Luckily the doctor heard the wagon and came out and helped him into the house.

"Where's Ann?" Dave said, sinking down on the sofa. The house seemed to be empty now except for Spinning and his wife.

"She went home. Mr. Gay took her. Borrowed my rig."

Dave was having a chill. He wondered if he could make it to the hotel. It came to him suddenly that he was very lucky not to have found Bart Hadder tonight.

"You're a sick man," Dr. Spinning said. "You're going to stay here tonight. The spare room is ready for you. I'll see to your horse."

Dave thought he had never heard sweeter words in his life.

It was daylight. He was buried in a huge bed. Every bone in his body ached but he thought he had got some of his strength back. Mrs. Spinning brought him an eggnog with a liberal portion of brandy in it. He slept until afternoon, when she brought him another eggnog and said he had a visitor. It was Holland Gay.

"Well, I give you fair warnin'," Holland said when they were alone. "Don't say I didn't."

"So it was you. You had me beaten up."

Holland giggled as if he had done something clever. "I didn't say that. I do say you're lucky. If it hadn't been for Ann, you'd of got worse 'n you did."

Dave didn't understand and said so.

"I guess you was too far gone to know she was there." Holland giggled again. "She went lookin' for you and she found them fellers kickin' the bejesus outen you. She screamed till some folks come a-runnin' from the dance.

"It give her quite a shock to have a feller take her to a dance and get the bejesus kicked outen him. She don't feel sorry for you, neither, like you might think she would. She said it served you right."

Dave sipped his eggnog, feeling the heat of the brandy. Trying to sound casual, he said, "Is Ann's Uncle Ben at Covey's?"

"Wasn't when I left there this noon. You goin' back there?"

"Certainly."

"So you ain't learned your lesson yet." Holland's merriment was gone, his voice shrill. "Well, go ahead. What you got last night is only a beginnin'. You'll get more and worse till you're outen this country. There ain't room for you in the Puyallup valley or in Steilacoom. That's the lesson you got to learn."

8

AFTER ANOTHER night's rest and a hearty breakfast at Spinning's, Dave shaved his bruised and swollen face, dressed, and drove to Covey's. He unhitched the horse and hung up the harness in the barn without seeing anyone. He found Ann and her father in the kitchen, washing dishes.

"Well, aren't you a sight!" Ann said with more reproach than sympathy in her tone.

Isaac Covey looked him over with something like amusement, then grew solemn. "We got sickness. Alice and Bobby come down with it and now Hannah's got it. Keeps Ann and me a-runnin'."

"What is it?"

"I reckon it's kind of the quinsy-like. Fever and chills and sore throats."

Dave helped dry the dishes and when they were finished Covey went into the front of the house. Ann said, "Let's go out on the porch," and he followed her there. She sat down on the wash bench. One of her braids had come unpinned and stuck out at a ridiculous angle. She looked tired.

"Is there anything I can do for you?" he said. "Go for a doctor?"

She met his eyes and said abruptly, "David, what do you want with Uncle Ben?"

"Who said I wanted him?"

"Well you do—that's why you're here. You're no homesteader."

"Think what you like."

"What did Uncle Ben do?"

He hesitated, leaning against the cedar column at the corner of the porch. Her questions irritated him. She was jumping to conclusions—and she was right. He decided that the best thing he could do now was to take her into his confidence. He took a deep breath and his broken rib sent a stab of pain through him.

"He killed a man. My brother Paul. It wasn't a fight or self-defense or anything like that. It was deliberate murder."

He told her all of it then: Bart Hadder's trial, his escape, the long search for him. She listened with her pretty face frozen into a shocked stare.

"Mother and Father know he's in some kind of trouble and changed his name. They don't know what. This will just about kill them."

"Did you tell them he was at the dance?" Dave asked.

"Yes, but that's all I said. I didn't say you started after him. You didn't find him, did you?"

He shook his head. "Ann, don't tell them any of this. Maybe they'll never have to know about him."

"I don't know *what* to do. I'm all mixed up."

"Promise me not to mention this to anybody," he persisted. "If you'll do that, I'll do my best to keep your folks from knowing the truth about Bart Hadder. I'm not sure I can do it, but I'll try."

"You're afraid somebody will warn him."

"Yes," he said, "I am."

"You don't care about anything else, do you? Just getting him." She tilted her chin at him as if defying him to deny it.

He moved away from the post and walked the length of the porch, wanting to get back to his claim. It was a warm day and the woods looked cool and restful. He turned back toward Ann.

"Paul and I were orphaned when he was fourteen and I was nine. He supported me. He even sent me to Jacksonville to college for a year. I always thought I'd pay him back some day, but I never settled down long enough to do it. A week before he was killed, I quit a job to go on a hunting trip. We had an argument about it and that was the last time I saw him alive. Now I'm doing something I think he'd want me to do. It isn't an easy thing . . . You might say I *can't* care about anything else until it's done."

Ann found the loose braid and pinned it in place.

"All right, David. I'll keep your secret. But I won't do anything to help you. Don't ask me." She held his eyes until he nodded and muttered, "Fair enough."

"David, those men who beat you had nothing to do with Uncle Ben, did they?"

"No."

"Holland had them do it, didn't he?"

"I expect so."

"It was an awful thing to do and I'm going to tell him so. But I'm not sorry for you. You don't want that claim. I kept telling myself you liked it and that you liked us as neighbors. I even thought you liked me. But you were just lying and pretending."

84

"I do like you."

"No. You're too filled up with hatred to like anybody."

He wanted to say this wasn't true, but it was a useless thing to argue about. What he was filled with was the need to finish the task he had laid out for himself; but she was partly right—there was hatred in him, too. He said, "Have it your way."

She got up from the bench and went to the door, turning with her hand on the latch as if waiting for him to say something more. Then she said, "David, I don't know what to do. I don't know if we need a doctor or not. Mother and Alice have got high fevers and it's hard for them to breathe. Bobby isn't so bad."

A sudden ugly thought came to him and he asked if he could see Alice. Ann led him through the house to a bedroom where the little girl lay half awake, flushed, breathing stridently. One glance and he was pretty sure it was diphtheria, which he had had when he was in his teens.

"She needs a doctor just as soon as we can get one here."

"I don't know," Isaac Covey said from the doorway. "I keep hoping they'll get better. I got no money—I wonder if the doctor will take one of them shoats."

Dave made the long walk to his claim, finding Tilluk there and everything as he had left it. He rested on his bunk while Tulluk caught the horse and saddled it; then he started back to Steilacoom, alternately walking and cantering the horse because at a trot the pain in his chest was unbearable.

Between the Fort and the town, he met the volunteer road gang on their way to begin work. They were a rough-looking, cheerful bunch, riding in a ragged column with their supplies on pack animals at the rear. Ed Allen, leader of the group, stopped Dave and tried to recruit him; but Dave's bandaged chest gave him a ready excuse and he laughed, saying, "If I swung an axe, it would kill me."

He pulled his horse off the road to make room for the column and watched it pass with impersonal interest. Farmers, storekeepers, mill owners, adventurers—these men were letting themselves in for the hardest kind of work and weeks in the woods without pay. But not without reward, he thought. They were going to make a dream come true.

Near the end of the group, he saw two men riding together who were carefully avoiding his gaze and he caught his breath. They were the pair who had beaten him. He had scarcely got a good look at them in the darkness in back of the warehouse and he was surprised to recognize them so easily; but there was no doubt in his mind and he felt the helpless anger of that night come back to him. He touched his holster with his elbow as he watched them pass, but he made no move to stop them.

He found Spinning at his blacksmith shop, fitting a tire on a wagon. When he had finished, the doctor changed his leather apron for a frock coat, saddled a horse, and they rode to Covey's together.

It turned out that Dave's guess had been right—

the Coveys had diphtheria. The doctor examined the three patients, swabbed their throats, and gave Ann a bottle of medicine for them before pronouncing the dreadful word. Bobby seemed to have a light case, he said, though he could get suddenly worse. Mrs. Covey and Alice were deathly ill.

9

THE NEXT TEN days were a nightmare for Ann.

Eight-year-old Ella came down with the disease the morning after the doctor's first visit, seeming to get sick just from the terrible knowledge that others were. Like Bobby, however, she had a fairly light case and after a few days her fever went down. Mrs. Covey needed constant attention, drifting in and out of a comatose sleep and wearing down her strength with worry and peevishness. Alice seemed the sickest, lying in a state of open-eyed listlessness and wasting away.

Ann was up a dozen times a night and she didn't take off her clothes for days at a time. She stretched out on her bed when she could and, listening to the rasping breathing of the two little girls in the bed next to hers, slept in snatches. Her father tried to relieve the strain on her but he tired easily; besides, she kept him away from the patients as much as she could because she was afraid he would get the disease.

At times—sometimes in the middle of the night—she had to get out of the house for a while and walked around the clearing or to the river bend, taking strength from the fresh air and the sight of healthy living things. Sometimes she was tempted to visit Dave's cabin, just to chat about nothing for a few minutes; but she always decided that the less she saw of him the better for her, and she never went there.

He showed up every day at the farm, however, asking what he could do. She thanked him politely and said there was nothing, though she would often see him later helping her father with what chores his broken rib would let him do. She accepted Holland Gay's help less reluctantly. It wasn't a matter of encouraging one and discouraging the other but of keeping her own feelings in check. She wasn't afraid of their getting out of control in regard to Holland.

Still, from an unemotional point of view, she was seeing Holland differently. At least, his motives were clear and she knew where she stood with him. And he made himself so useful that at times she wondered what she would do without him. He paid the doctor bills, rode clear to Olympia for a special medicine the doctor wanted, brought presents of fruit and food, and several times brought out a woman to relieve Ann for an afternoon. He did these things cheerfully, glad of a chance to please her. For the first time, she could think of him as being genuinely fond of her instead of merely wanting to own her as he might a horse or a piece of land. He seemed to be capable of something like devotion—and that made up for a lot of his bad qualities.

She had set her cap for David—rather shamelessly, she thought. Now she knew he didn't want her. All he wanted was Uncle Ben hanged—that was David, that was his life. He had been bad for her because he had made her think of the romantic things a girl wants in a man—the things Holland Gay didn't have. But at a time like this, when hardship came, you realized there were other considerations. It would make up for a lot of lost romance to have a home you weren't always in danger of losing because of debt, to have children who weren't raised in poverty as she had been, to be able to send for a doctor when you needed one without having to stop and reckon how you'd pay him.

Dr. Spinning came every second day, doing what he could, showing her how to swab throats and sponge down fever, telling her she was a good nurse but should get more rest. He was always cheerful but at the same time tried to prepare her and her father for the worst. One rainy afternoon when the sickness had been with them a week, he called them into the kitchen.

"Alice isn't making it," he said. "Unless she has a sudden rally in the next few hours, she'll go. I've done everything I can."

That night Ann sat beside the girls' bed, sponging Alice's face, trying to get her to take some nourishment. She sat in the dark because a lamp or candle seemed to burn all the freshness out of the air. At last she dozed—and woke knowing something was different, something was wrong. She listened to the awful breathing from the bed and, horrified, realized that only Ella was breathing. Alice was dead.

She got a lantern and went to the barn, where her father lay open-eyed on the bunk, and told him. He lay still with his eyes glassy in the weird light. For a long time he was silent, then he said, "We got to get her outen that bed. Can't have Ella wake up and find her."

They went to the house and wrapped the body in a blanket and brought it to the barn. Isaac Covey laid it gently on the bunk. "We'll say nothing of this to Hannah till she's better. . . . I'll build a coffin in the morning. We'll bury her in that grassy place on the far side of the pasture. I'll build a little fence around it and it'll be a little cemetery, the beginning of a family cemetery."

As they walked back to the house he said, "Ann, I got to keep this place, no matter what. With my own flesh and blood buried on it, I got to keep it."

She made coffee and they sat helplessly at the kitchen table. Toward morning she fell asleep with her head on her arms. She woke to her father's gentle shaking.

"Hannah wants you. She's bad."

Ann lighted a candle and went into her stepmother's bedroom. Mrs. Covey's eyes turned briefly toward her and rolled back to stare upward at nothing. Her voice was so low and harsh that Ann didn't realize for a moment that she was speaking.

"Ike wouldn't say yes or no, but I want a clear answer from you. Alice is gone, ain't she?"

Ann sighed and fought back tears. "She died in her sleep."

"I want to be buried with her in a double grave."

"Mother! You're going to get well."

"Don't waste my strength arguin'. A double grave, do you hear? Our coffins touchin'. Get a preacher if you can find one. Get him to say a few words over us."

"Yes, Mother. We'll find one."

"You got to take care of your father, and Bobby and Ella if they live. It's all on your shoulders. There's somethin' you got to promise me."

"All right."

"You got to marry Holland. Promise me."

She isn't going to die, Ann thought. *She's better and she's doing this to get her way. I'll promise and when she's well I'll tell her it isn't binding because she didn't die.*

Still, she hesitated.

"It's the only thing," Mrs. Covey said. "It's the only way to get Ike clear. I can't rest till you promise."

"If he asks me again," Ann said.

"He'll ask you again." Mrs. Covey's eyes rolled toward Ann again. "You promised, now. Some day you'll thank me I made you promise. You promised, didn't you?"

"Yes."

"Write to Ben—your Uncle Ben. I loaned him some money I had stashed away. Nineteen dollars. Ike don't know nothin' about it. You write to Ben and let him know you know he owes it. He's doin' well now and he can pay it."

"Where do I write to him?"

"Mr. Benjamin Weller, Port Townsend. They'll

keep the letter at the post office till he calls for it . . . I can rest now, knowin' you promised."

She closed her eyes. She was unconscious all the next day and died that evening.

Mother and daughter were buried according to Mrs. Covey's wishes, in a double grave with the coffins touching. A few neighbors were there (the nearest lived four miles down the valley), bringing wildflowers to strew on the coffins and gifts of food for the bereaved family. The only ceremony was at the graveside, in spite of a drizzling rain, and was conducted by an earnest young minister that Holland Gay had brought all the way from Olympia. When the coffins had been lowered, he led them in a song they all knew—

> *I came to the place where the white pilgrim lay,*
> *And pensively stood by his tomb,*
> *When in a low whisper I heard something say,*
> *"How sweetly I sleep here alone."*

Holland Gay and Dave, in spite of his broken rib, began to fill in the grave and the others walked back to the house. When the visitors had left and Ann and her father were standing alone with the minister on the porch, he asked if they would bow their heads and pray with him; but Isaac Covey turned abruptly away and went back to help with filling the grave and to put up the slab into which he had lovingly burned names and dates with a poker:

HANNAH H. COVEY

1815 — 1853

ALICE

1847 — 1853

AT PEECE

Nobody had the heart to correct his spelling.

Bobby had had to be told the tragic news when he heard the visitors' voices; Ella had slept through the funeral and still didn't know her mother and sister were dead. After Holland had left with the minister Ann went into the bedroom and found her awake.

"Where *is* Alice?" Ella demanded.

Then, at last, Ann gave way to tears.

10

DAVE KEPT Tilluk in his employ, letting him clear land in back of his cabin and paying him in clothing, powder and shot, matches, fishhooks. Nippin's Indians were busy at the same work and had made considerable headway against the forest in the direction of the river. One morning when they felled a giant fir, the top of Mount Tacoma came into sight like a great white jewel above the other trees. Tilluk hailed this as a good omen. At any rate, it made a grand view from Dave's cabin and he considered that the claim jumper had done him a real favor.

His rib knitted quickly and he could soon ride without discomfort. He visited the land office at Olympia, showing his letter from the Governor of Oregon Territory, and was permitted to examine the files of claim holders. He was hoping to find one in the name of Ben Weller, but he did not. He asked cautious questions at two lumber mills near Olympia, too, and learned that Weller occasionally acted as agent for one of them; but the owner could give little more information than DeLin about the man's headquarters.

"I suppose you'd be more likely to run into him at Port Townsend than anywhere else," he said. "That's the port of entry for the Sound and I'd think it would be the place for him to meet sea captains looking for lumber."

After that, Dave boarded ships that were in port at Olympia and Steilacoom and questioned the captains. Some of them knew Weller, had even had him aboard. When Dave discovered that there was often a card game in the captain's cabin, he was certain that DeLin had been right—being agent for lumber mills was not a living for Ben Weller (as Dave now thought of him). It merely gave him an excuse to make contact with sea captains and mill owners, and a mantle of respectability while he bilked them at the card table.

Port Townsend was seventy-five miles north of Steilacoom by water. Dave did not immediately undertake a trip there because, after the deaths of Mrs. Covey and Alice, he thought it probable that Weller would soon visit his sister's family. He fell into the habit of checking the Covey pasture several times a day for a strange horse. One afternoon late in August, however, something happened that took him out of the valley for a few days.

He was helping Tilluk with the clearing, swinging an axe without discomfort for the first time, when a redheaded young man rode into the meadow. Dave recognizing him as Andy Burge, who was in charge of getting supplies to the road gang.

"I've got a pack train of ten horses," Burge said, swinging down from his horse and shaking hands. "My helper got thrown when he tried to cross the river. Wrenched his shoulder and had to turn back. Can you help me take the train through? These supplies are late now and the camp must be running low."

"How long will the trip take?"

"Three-four days. Not more than that. You're my last hope, Porter. If you turn me down, I'll have to try it alone."

Dave remembered how the trail wound back and forth across the S'Kamish. The road makers would have eliminated some of those twenty-odd crossings but not all of them. For one man to get ten horses through seemed next to impossible. Dave thought of sending Tilluk, but he knew the Puyallups had a superstitious dread of going near the mountain. Besides, there was the score he had to settle with two men at the road gang's camp.

"Where's your train now?"

"At the ford below Covey's. Had to leave 'em alone. If half of 'em aren't trying to rub off their packs by now, I'm lucky."

"I'll meet you there in half an hour," Dave said.

Burge rode off then. Dave called to Tilluk and gave him instructions to watch the Covey farm while he was gone. He described Weller's appearance as accurately as he could in Chinook.

"If this man comes and goes away, follow him. Even if he goes across water, hire a canoe and follow him. Send word to me where you are, but stay with him. Here is money you'll need if this happens. I haven't much money left; so be careful of it."

Andy Burge made a good traveling companion. He knew horses and he knew the woods. He was an energetic man, both high-spirited and earnest, talking as if the trip were a joke and yet knowing every detail about every horse.

They reached the S'Kamish that evening and camped on the near bank, waiting a while before removing the packs from the horses so as to let them cool down slowly. By the time they had rubbed down the animals and staked them for the night, it was pitch-dark. They could have kept two or three more men busy.

The next morning, they followed the new road, which was merely a swath in the forest. At one point where an eight-foot trunk lay across the path, the road makers had tunneled under it rather than cut through it or swerve the road around it. At other places the way was so tortuous and narrow that there seemed to be barely room for a wagon to scrape through. There was little evidence of grading—the road bed was merely the soft forest floor with its roots and hollows, sloughs and knolls.

"I guess it's wide enough to get a wagon *through*, all right," Burge said, "but how anybody is going to get one *over* it is beyond me. . . . Well, I guess they figure on slashing it out as quick as they can and improving it later."

The number of fordings had been reduced to sixteen; but to get the pack train across, Dave and Burge had to ride back and forth several times at each one. Even though the river was low, half a dozen horses lost their footing at one time and another, floundering in terror, wetting rope and blanket and canvas to make their packs heavier and chafe their backs.

They reached the camp about four in the afternoon, a haphazard cluster of tents and lean-tos on a little creek that emptied into the Greenwater River. Only the cook was there, impaling great chunks of venison on improvised spits. When they had staked the horses, they built a fire and dried their clothes.

After sundown the workers began to straggle in, axes and cant hooks on their shoulders. Dave sat against a tree behind his fire and watched for his two men. They came in together and joined a group at the creek that was washing up. They didn't notice Dave.

He got up and went up behind the larger of the two, who was kneeling and washing his face. Dave seized him by the back of his shirt collar, pulling him to his feet, and hit him in the face with all his strength. He spun, staggered and fell. He got to his knees with his nose between his hands.

"You bust my nose," he mumbled. Blood colored his palms and wound down his wrists.

"Get up," Dave said.

"I ain't goin' to fight you with my nose bust."

Dave pulled him to his feet, knocked his hands away from his face, and saw that his nose was indeed broken. The man made no resistance but just stood their pathetically, looking like a child about to cry. "I reckon you're even with me," he whined. Dave thrust him away disgustedly.

Men were standing around open-mouthed; others were running up from all parts of the camp. Dave didn't see the other man he wanted. Ed Allen strode up angrily.

"What do you mean by starting a fight in camp? Don't you know better than that?"

"Sorry, but this can't wait."

"Look out!" Allen shoved Dave and spun him around to face the man who was coming up behind him with the end of a logging chain raised like a blackjack. It was the second man of the pair.

"Rufe!" Allen bellowed. "Drop that chain!"

The man made a rush for Dave, but Allen, who was powerfully built, intercepted him, seizing his wrists and bending his arms back until he let go of the chain.

"I want no more of this!" Allen said, releasing Rufe with a shove.

Rufe made a dash for a log a few yards away where some of the men had left their axes. He seized one of these and advanced with it at port arms.

"I'll part the hair of any son of a bitch as gets in my way," he screamed. He was half crazy with fear and excitement.

"Some of you men help me get that axe!" Allen said.

"Stand back!" Dave said, picking up the logging chain. His voice stopped the three or four men who had started forward. Even Allen stepped out of the way.

It was an eight-foot chain and he doubled it. Holding it by the center, he whirled it around his head, took a step toward the advancing Rufe and swung the chain at him like a whip. Rufe sidestepped and threw up the axe to protect his head. The ends of the chain hit the axe handle harmlessly.

Rufe charged. Dave danced backward, whirling the chain, then suddenly lunged forward. This time he let go of the chain and followed it in. It flew around the axe and struck Rufe in the face—not a crippling blow but one that took off some skin, forced him to duck and dodge at the same time, and threw him off balance. Dave seized the axe with one hand just below the head and the other near the end of the handle. He forced the double-bitted head slowly toward Rufe's face; then, taking advantage of Rufe's resisting pressure, he suddenly let the head come forward past his shoulder and crashed the end of the handle against Rufe's jaw. Rufe sagged to his knees, leaving Dave standing over him with the axe in his hands.

Dave flung the axe aside and pulled the dazed Rufe to his feet. Seized by a sudden cruel impulse, he broke the man's nose with a short right hook and left him moaning on the ground.

The men made way for him without comments or congratulations or even attempts at humor. They were rough men who would revel in his cruelty eventually as they told and retold the story, but for this moment they were shocked by it. He went to his fire and sat alone. In a little while Ed Allen came over.

"Those were the men who gave you a going-over the night of the dance; I know all about that. Now your score is settled. Do you feel better?"

"Some."

"I'll probably lose them both now. How about taking the place of one of them?"

"I've got to get back."

"You've got a claim, haven't you?" Allen said.

Dave nodded.

"I don't like to tell a man what to do, but nothing in your life is more important than this road."

"Sorry," Dave said.

He slept badly that night. He was annoyed with Allen, though it was natural for the man to assume he was a homesteader and had an interest in seeing the road finished. Mostly he was dissatisfied with himself. He'd come to this camp to settle a score when he should have stayed near Covey's. He'd settled it in a brutal way that men would remember but that he was ashamed of now. And what had he settled?

Would it be any different when he had taken Ben Weller and sent him off to hang? Weller was a killer who would probably kill again if he weren't removed from society; but Dave knew it would be a hypocrisy to pretend his main interest was in protecting society. His search for Weller was a search for revenge, personal and cruel. He would take him or die trying, but what would he have when he took him? And what would come next—another score to settle? It would be easy enough to spend your life settling scores, large and small, if your life had no special direction to it . . . At last he drifted into a restless sleep in which a primitive fear of the night took hold of him. More than once he wrenched himself awake with the thought that an enemy crept up to split his head with an axe.

He and Burge spent the next day packing equipment to points up the trail where Allen intended to establish future camps. It was tedious work and he chafed to get back to his claim. They camped alone that night not far from the place where he had been surprised by the Klikitats. While they were cooking their bacon and beans, they had a visitor, a boy with a message from east of the mountains: word had been relayed from Fort Hall that a wagon train resting there had decided to take the new road to the Sound. The boy was headed for Allen's camp; but when he learned that Dave and Burge were going back in the morning, he turned back eastward and left them to carry the news.

The camp greeted it with cheers, but Allen was solemn.

"Fort Hall is roughly six hundred miles and thirty days by ox team away," he said. "We won't have much of a road in that time. Well, we'll do the best we can for them, but they'll have to do a little chopping as they come."

It was a cool, summer morning with the forest dripping from a recent rain when Dave left Burge on the Steilacoom road and took the branch that led to his claim. When he rode into the Covey clearing, Isaac Covey was loading bags of wheat on the wagon and Ann was sweeping the porch. She returned his wave without enthusiasm and turned away. It was a discouraging greeting but he rode over anyway and gave her the news about the wagon train.

She said, "Is that so?" uninterestedly and then, "That *is* wonderful news. It will do us all good." It seemed to Dave that she wanted to be excited but wasn't because she had something else very much on her mind.

Isaac Covey reacted differently, letting out a war whoop, shaking Dave's hand and saying it was the best news he'd ever had. Then he sobered.

"I wish I could tell you somethin' good in return," he said. "But I can't. Fact is, I don't rightly know how to speak about it. Your cabin's gone."

"Gone?"

"Burned. Clean to the ground. It ain't for me to say how."

11

HE SAT HIS HORSE looking at the gray-and-black rubble with a growing emptiness that was like a sickness. The cabin was close to a total loss. Some of the logs were merely charred but they were strewed about as if somebody had pulled down walls that were left standing. Even the stone chimney had toppled and shattered. He glanced across the meadow and saw Nippin watching him, rifle under his arm. He rode over.

"You did it," Dave said. "You sneaking little bastard."

"Lightnin' struck it," Nippin said happily, his words thickened by a wad of tobacco. "Made a right pretty blaze. Lucky the woods was wet or they might of caught. Well, I told you I'd outstay you."

There was an axe leaning against Nippin's cabin. Dave rode over and picked it up and saw it was his own. Nippin watched him examine it.

"Well, you owed me an axe for the one you shot up," Nippin said.

"What else of mine have you got?"

"Nothin'."

Dave got off his horse. "I'll have a look."

Nippin leveled the rifle. "You stay outen that cabin. Do as I say now or I'll smoke you."

"No you won't. Holland Gay doesn't want you mixed up in a killing. If that weren't so, you'd have got me long ago."

He went into the cabin and found other things that were his—a dutch oven, a knife, twenty rounds for his revolver, a shirt. Nippin stood in the doorway, indecision in his twisted face. Finally his mean humor prevailed.

"You ought to thank me for savin' them things for you." He backed off to let Dave leave.

Dave led his horse across the meadow and turned it to graze. He went into the wood and found the hut where Tilluk slept, a dry, cozy shelter of poles and boughs. Tilluk was nowhere around.

It all added up. Ben Weller must have visited the Coveys. Tilluk had followed him when he left. The Indian's absence had given Nippin his chance to fire the cabin. There was nothing to do but stay close to the claim until he heard from Tilluk.

He worked all morning building a hut of his own, hiding it in the brush at the edge of the woods so he could watch Nippin's cabin without being seen. He worked hard, trying not to think, trying to burn away some of the anger that threatened to consume him. Toward noon, he walked to Covey's.

Ann met him at the back door. Her father had taken a load of wheat to the mill at Steilacoom, she said, and the children had gone with him.

"I have no food," Dave said. "I came to borrow flour, bacon, coffee—anything you can spare. I'll pay you back as soon as I can get to town."

"Surely." She went into the house, closing the

door and leaving him on the porch. After a moment he followed her.

She glided about the kitchen, collecting staples he would need and putting them into a flour sack. She said politely, "I'm sorry about your cabin."

"Sorry? I thought you'd say it served me right."

"All right then—I'm not sorry. I don't care one way or the other. I just don't care, David!" She stopped in the middle of the room, slender and graceful and with her eyes boring into him, demanding a reaction from him. She didn't realize that by making her words seem so important to her she was taking the sting out of them.

"I'm going to build another cabin," he said, making the decision then and there.

"Are you? Why? You'll never prove up on that place."

He wanted to say no, but he was going to get Nippin off it and sell his rights; but that would make her more antagonistic than ever.

"I might," he said.

"You're pretending again."

He grinned. "You want to argue, don't you?"

"You started it," she said, tipping her chin.

She was still facing him, holding the sack of food in front of her. He stepped over and took it and laid it on the table. Deliberately, he put his hands against her back and drew her to him and kissed her. Her arms slid around his neck and they kissed for a long time.

She pushed away and he let her go. She sat down at the kitchen table.

"We shouldn't have done that," she said. "I don't want that. Not ever again."

"Ann—" he began, not knowing what he wanted to say. He bent over her chair and tried to kiss her again and was surprised by the force with which she tore away from him and by the anger in her face.

"Not *ever* again!" After a moment she said softly, "There's your food. You'd best go."

He wanted her, wanted to hold her again, but he saw he couldn't touch her without making a brute or a beggar of himself. He settled the food in the sack, swung it over his shoulder, and said the worst possible thing."

"When was your Uncle Ben here?"

Her brown eyes were startled. Then she sighed. "So we're back to Uncle Ben. Is that why you kissed me? So I'd tell you about him?"

"You know it wasn't."

"No, I don't know!"

"I kissed you because I wanted to and you wanted me to. Maybe it didn't mean any more than that. Maybe it did. To both of us. We ought to find out."

She thought that over, studying him. "I've already found out, David. It didn't mean anything except I can't believe you. I can't believe anything you say—or do."

"I can't change that by arguing about it. Thanks for the food."

"Don't forget your gun." She pointed to the carbine he had left standing by the door. She added fiercely, "You won't need to bring it when you

108

come here after this. I'm sure Uncle Ben won't be back for a long time."

"You warned him!"

She didn't reply at once, plainly enjoying his anxiety. Finally she smiled and said in a tone she might use to a trying child. "No, David. I told you I'd keep your secret and I did. But I made him feel unwelcome. I told him he couldn't stay because Holland Gay was coming and was going to sleep in the barn. And I made him give me nineteen dollars he owed Mother. I was kind of huffy about it."

"When was he here?"

"I'm not going to tell you anything that might help you."

She raised her chin in the stubborn way she had, and he had to grin, thinking he might as well go and question a fence post.

That afternoon he put a crew of Indians to work cutting logs for a new cabin, though he took little interest in the work and did none of it himself. The next two days he waited lazily for word from Tilluk, smoking too much, watching Nippin and trying to think of a way of getting rid of him without shooting him. The trouble was that the man was never without his rifle. No doubt he slept with it.

As soon as he saw the Indians at work, Nippin began his senseless shooting again, doing his best to make life miserable for everybody on that side of the meadow. When Dave carelessly left his saddle in sight and later found it torn by two bullets, he thought for a moment that he would shoot it out with the twisted little man after all; but he smothered his temper and even pretended to laugh off the damage when the Indians discovered it.

The next morning he at last got his chance at the man.

Nippin had no well but used the turbid glacial water from the river, letting it stand until some of the sediment settled. He usually sent an Indian to get it, but this morning Dave saw him start out with a bucket in each hand and the ever present rifle held awkwardly under an arm.

Dave left his guns in the hut and raced along the trail he had cut to the river. At the bank he turned upstream to the place where Nippin's trail came out. Puffing, he knelt behind a clump of saplings and watched the trail through their lower branches. Almost at once he heard Nippin coming, his buckets creaking on their handles; then the red-shirted little man ambled into sight and stopped on the bank a scant ten feet away.

Nippin set one bucket on the bank and leaned his rifle against a tree. He climbed gingerly down the four-foot bank with the other bucket. Dave strode over and got the rifle. Nippin was below him on a narrow strip of beach, filling the bucket, and didn't see him. Dave fired both barrels in the air.

Nippin whirled around terrified, dropping the bucket. "Now—" he stammered, "now—now—"

Dave tossed the rifle far into the raging gray water. He jumped down to the beach, blocked a clumsy blow, grabbed Nippin and spun him around.

He placed a foot against the man's buttocks and kicked him into the river.

The water was scarcely three feet deep here, but it was swift and the bottom was rocky and uneven. Nippin came up five yards downstream, went under again, finally got his feet under him. He stood still a moment, choking and spitting, then began to work his way toward the bank. Dave met him and kicked him into the water again.

For a long moment, the man was out of sight and Dave had a sudden sick feeling. Then the red undershirt appeared in shallow water near a rocky little shoal and Nippin raised his head. He got slowly to his feet and waded to the shoal, where the water was only a few inches deep. He was half drowned but when he saw Dave wading out to him he picked up a stone and hurled it, missing widely. The effort cost him his balance and he sat down in the shallow water. Dave pulled him to his feet.

"I'm going to drown you."

Nippin tried to grin as if it were all a joke. He gasped something unintelligible.

"Your body will wash up on a bar somewhere," Dave said. "Or maybe it will be carried clear to the Sound and left on a beach by the tide. Nobody will blame me for it."

"No need—to do that. I'll get offen the claim. That's—what you want."

Dave turned him around to face the deep water beyond the shoal. There was a long sweep of plunging water here where even a good swimmer wouldn't have much chance.

"This way I'll be sure."

"I'll leave, Porter. You can be sure."

"Can you write?"

"Not real good. I can write my name though."

"Will you sign a statement that Holland Gay paid you to jump my claim?"

"If you say so."

They went back to Nippin's cabin and he got into dry clothes. He was exhausted—and obliging. Dave helped him pack his meager belongings, finding more of his own things among them.

"I wouldn't of stayed the winter anyways," Nippin said. "Holland Gay didn't pay me nothin'—just my food and junk for the Injuns and a quart of whisky a week. He said he'd give me fifty dollars when you got off."

"Did he tell you to fire the cabin?"

"Yes sir. He said to do it first chance I got when you was gone and the woods was wet."

"We'll put all that in the statement," Dave said.

They threw everything that belonged to Holland Gay into a tarpaulin and carried it to Covey's on a pole between their horses. Isaac Covey said they could leave it in a corner of the barn, and the whole family came out to watch them tote it in. Ann demanded to know what had happened.

"Mr. Nippin is leaving," Dave said. He thought she looked happy in spite of her frown.

"I reckon I don't want to live so dang close to a river," Nippin said, his sarcasm taking a humble twist.

They left at once for Steilacoom, making the long

ride without conversation. Dave found a lawyer, who called in witnesses and prepared to write down Nippin's statement. For a moment, Nippin seemed on the verge of balking, but he did not.

"You could just as well of drownded me," he said; "so I reckon I'll go through with it. But you got to promise you won't get me in no trouble with the law."

He told the whole story, saying he had been put on the claim by Holland Gay and promised fifty dollars to get Dave off. He had agreed to sign over his rights when Holland had sold his Fox Island claim and was eligible to take another. He had burned Dave's cabin at Holland's instigation.

"This is a damaging document," the lawyer said as the witnesses were signing. "It's grounds for a criminal prosecution of Gay if you want that."

"I'd prosecute with pleasure," Dave said, "but I can't spare the time."

"I don't think you'll be bothered by Gay again—not if he knows we have this."

"I'll see that he knows it."

Dave knew that the witnesses would probably have the story all over town by evening, but he took steps to get it to Holland Gay at once. As they left the office, he gave Nippin a dollar.

"Buy a drink in Holland Gay's saloon. Tell him what happened. All of it."

Nippin grinned. "I'll talk fast and get out quick."

Dave put Nippin's Indians to work with his own and went to work himself. The next day they got the roof on his cabin. He enlarged the doorway in the cabin across the meadow and used it to stable his horse, thinking that the claim now ought to be worth three hundred dollars at least. Maybe more.

There was a new satisfaction in the meadow, now that he had it all to himself. He caught himself just standing and looking at it sometimes, hearing the liturgy of the river and feeling the peacefulness of the sun-yellowed grass and the soft forest wall with the opalescent crown of the mountain above it. These things were his, he thought. And sometimes they were more than his; sometimes they were part of his being and he of theirs.

Yet he was also often uneasy under the spell of the meadow and wished he were not so closely bound to it until he heard from Tilluk. He was afraid of its growing hold on him, afraid of the hurt of parting from it. Most of all, he was afraid of its ultimate cost to him. For, in spite of what the lawyer had said, he knew Holland Gay would go on fighting him—or hiring others to do his vicious fighting for him.

12

IT WAS a mild evening with the stars out clear and she was walking along the road with Holland. This was going to be the night; she wasn't going to put it off again; she was going to see that it happened. She was as ready for it as she ever would be and she knew just what she was going to say.

Holland was still dreadfully upset about losing the claim and was talking, as usual, in bursts. It was as if he took a moment to think up some harsh thing about David and then believed he made it true just by saying it.

"He beat up a poor Injun in Steilacoom and robbed him of his money. . . . He beat up two fellers up to the road camp. Busted their noses just for the fun of it."

She had heard these things before from Holland and she had heard different versions of them from her father. David was a hard one, all right; but she knew it was his own money he had taken from the Indian and she knew the men with the broken noses were the ones Holland had paid to thrash David at the dance. She could argue with Holland, she thought. It would take up time and he would turn sullen and probably wouldn't kiss her and ask her to marry him. But that wouldn't be getting it over with.

"He has a squaw in Steilacoom," Holland said,

glancing slyly at her. "Any white man who'd live with a squaw is a scum."

"Father says it isn't true about the squaw. He asked Mr. Balch, who knows everything about everybody."

"It is so true. I seen her."

"Is she a flathead?"

"No siree! She's pretty as a picture."

It always nettled her to hear about the squaw. She wouldn't put it past David to have a squaw. She wouldn't put anything past him.

"This country would be better off without scum like him," Holland said.

"Yes, it would."

It pleased him to have her agree. She walked close to him so their arms brushed. In a moment he reached down and took her hand and she knew he had stopped thinking about David. He was thinking about kissing her and pretty soon now he would do it—about when they got to the bottom of the hollow that lay ahead.

He was a little backward in the kissing department. He seemed to consider a kiss a somewhat silly preliminary to the passionate love-making he wanted and that she wouldn't allow. Sometimes after kissing her he would suddenly do things that were downright crude, and sometimes he was hard to discourage. But tonight, after the first self-conscious effort, he seemed to take more pleasure in the kissing. It wasn't like when David had kissed her, but she stood against him and felt his excitement and felt vaguely excited herself and told herself it was nice.

"I reckon you know what's on my mind," he said.

"What, Holland?"

"I ain't a man of easy words and fine manners. But I'm fond of you and I'll do my best for you."

"Are you asking me again to marry you?"

"Let's do it right away."

"Not right away."

"When?"

"How about New Year's Day, Holland? That's less than four months away, do you realize that?"

He sighed noisily. "It's up to you, I guess. But them notes your father owes me is due in two months. If we ain't married by then, I will foreclose. I don't like to do it, but some things is business, Ann."

"How much does he owe you?"

"Four hundred and sixty-two dollars."

They had been on the claim more than three years and the rights, buildings and animals were surely worth more than that. Still, she knew her father had the crops mortgaged besides and didn't have a chance of raising four hundred and sixty-two dollars this year. She didn't see how he could get himself into such a preposterous mess.

"You give him more time, Holland. I'll marry you and it will be all in the family."

"No siree! I'll take the place. He can live on it and work it and pay me slow as he pleases. When he's paid up, I'll sign it back to him. But it's goin' into my name in two months. Unlessen we're married."

He knows I don't care anything about him, she

thought. He knows his hold on me is that debt. Why does he want me then? I shouldn't think he'd want me.

"There's this," Holland said. "Rightly speakin', that farm ain't a property. It's a claim. If I take over your father's rights, I'll have to move onto the place to keep 'em. So even if you don't marry me right away, I'm a-goin' to move in on you. Seems to me we best git married."

So that was how he had worked it out. Whether she married him or not, he was going to move in and become one of the family. She could see him gradually taking over, making the decisions, becoming the big duck in the puddle and turning her father into a sort of hired hand on his own land. The thought infuriated her, but she forced herself to be amiable.

He kissed her again. He slid his hands down her back to her buttocks. He held her tight against him and said, "Let's go sit on that log."

She wanted to say no, to scream it at him, but she murmured "All right," He led her to a big cedar log that lay along the roadside, lifted her up on it, and scrambled up beside her. He put an arm around her.

"I want to talk," she said.

"Go ahead and talk."

"If I promise to marry you in two months, will you give Father more time?"

"I reckon so. One year anyways."

"Well, I guess we could do it. If you'll get the papers fixed tomorrow."

"No siree. I'll do it after we get married."

"You don't trust me," she said. "You're afraid

I'll back out after you fix the papers. I won't, Holland. If I say I'll marry you in two months, I will."

"Some things is business, that's all."

"Well, I'm not going to marry a man who doesn't trust me."

He blinked at that for a while and then giggled. "You don't understand business."

"I understand this much. If you don't trust me, why should I trust you? How do I know you'll give Father more time if you don't fix the papers before we're married?"

He squeezed her and tried to pull her against him. "We'll talk later."

"No siree!" she said. "We'll have an understanding about this right now. Holland, you promise me you'll fix those papers tomorrow!"

He thought a long time, blinking and looking at his feet. After a while, he smiled faintly, as if amused by his thoughts. She knew he was thinking she was unreasonable and she also knew he would agree to fix the papers. He wants me awful bad, she thought. More than anything else. That's something to be thankful for.

"If you want me to, I will," he said. "It ain't good business, but I'm fond of you and I'll do the best I can for you."

"Thank you, Holland.'

"We'll get married right away."

"Let's make it two months from today," she said.

They sealed the bargain with a kiss. Then his stubby hands became possessive of her body. She let him have his way for a while, let his caresses excite her and was glad she could react that way. Then she suddenly slid off the log and began to walk back toward the farm. He caught her and hugged her.

"We're not married *yet*," she laughed. She wouldn't return his passion and he finally became discouraged and let her push away. He took her hand and they strolled leisurely homeward.

They found Isaac Covey sitting by a lamp in the front room, reading the Olympia newspaper. Bobby sat on the floor, braiding a whip out of rawhide. Ella had gone to bed.

Ann whispered to Holland, who drew himself up proudly and told the news.

"I and Ann have the pleasure to announce we are agreed to be man and wife. With your permission, Ike, the weddin' will transpire two months from today."

Isaac Covey stood up and Ann flung herself into his arms. He shook Holland's hand and said, "I'm glad it's settled."

Bobby stopped his braiding and watched soberly. Ann said, "Bobby, come over and kiss me and shake hands with Holland." Bobby threw aside his work and darted out of the house.

In a little while Holland went to the barn to bed, saying he wanted to get an early start to Steilacoom in the morning. When he had gone, Ann told her father he had agreed to extend the mortgages the next day. Isaac Covey slumped in his chair as if he didn't know whether to be pleased or sorry.

"You should of left me worry about that matter," he said.

"I could do better than you. I'm the one he wants to marry."

"You sure he's what *you* want?"

"Yes."

"Well, I want you to be sure. You don't have to marry him if you ain't sure."

Yes, I do, she thought. *You know it, Holland knows it, I know it. I'm going to make the best of it and not feel sorry for myself; but I wish we could all stop pretending and treat it like the business deal it is.*

"There's young Porter. I thought for a while you had a itch for him," her father said.

"No."

For some reason, denying it made her feel better. She went to bed hoping she could sleep, but she could not. She tried not to think, not to feel sorry for herself, not to puzzle about David. But as soon as she began to doze she lost control of her will, and her misery came back with a shock. After a while she began to sob. Ella heard her from the other bed and called to her in alarm. Ann got up and calmed her and got in bed with her until she fell asleep.

As the night wore on, she sought consolation by thinking about fate. Things happened as they were meant to happen. You thought you were deciding and planning and making things happen, but you weren't. You acted as you were meant to act.

She let her imagination go then, thinking of all the unlikely things that could happen in the next sixty days to change her fate. A crazy thought came to her and she knew at once it was going to be more than a thought. It was what she was meant to do. She would have her life with Holland, good or bad, but there was another life meant for her, too, a life separate and distinct and only a few hours long; but it would be all the things that life with Holland wouldn't be.

Almost without knowing she was doing it, she got out of bed and into her dress. She stepped into a pair of mocassins, threw a shawl over her shoulders, and tiptoed into the living room. Bobby had come in unnoticed and was asleep on the couch. She could hear her father snoring in the other bedroom. She stole through the kitchen, lifted up on the back door so it wouldn't creak as she opened it, and went out. She didn't dare take a lantern for fear Holland would see it from the barn.

A white moon had risen above the ragged blackness of the treetops and the night was liquid with shimmering foliage and flowing shadows. She walked swiftly along the wheat field to the woods, not thinking, letting herself be carried along by fate. She entered the black tunnel that was the trail to the river, wishing for the protection of a lantern now but thinking that if a bear got her, well, that would be fate too.

She stood before the rough, split-pole door of the new cabin and pounded on it. It opened just a crack, then wide. David faced her in blue flannel underwear, his eyes wide with astonishment, a cocked revolver in his hand. He looked so ridiculous that she had to laugh.

"What's wrong?" he demanded.

"David, let me come in."

He stepped back and got a lamp and lit it. She went in and closed the door. The cabin was bare except for a table, two stools and a bed. She sat down on one of the stools, finding it a little wobbly on the uneven dirt floor. She met his eyes and smiled to reassure him.

"David, I just have to talk to you, that's all. I haven't anyone else to talk to."

He looked more alarmed than ever, then laughed and smoothed back his hair. "You're crazy to come here at this time of night."

"I know it."

He took a pair of trousers from a peg in the wall, pulled them on, and sat across the table from her.

"It's a nice cabin," she said. "You certainly built it quick."

They chatted about the cabin, but she hardly heard what he said. She was deliciously comfortable just sitting there waiting for him to get over his surprise and be at ease. After a while she got up and went to the bed and sat on it, bouncing a little on the rope springs as if to try it for softness. He watched her silently, then came to her and bent over her and kissed her.

"David, this is just for tonight. Do you understand?"

"No."

"Tonight I promised to marry Holland."

"You don't love Holland. You even dislike him."

"I like him very much," she said emphatically. "I'm going to marry him and nothing is going to change that. That's why I came here. Do you understand?"

He laughed and shook his head. "I think you're completely crazy. You've done something that will hurt you."

"David, there's only tonight. Tonight is separate from all the rest of my life. If you don't understand that, don't talk about it. Just hold me."

He knelt beside her and kissed her and buried his head against her. He pushed her gently back on the bed and got up to blow out the lamp. She lay waiting for him in utter darkness, breathing deeply of the fragrance of fir and cedar and coal oil, feeling the delicate touch of the night breeze from the cabin door. And then his long body was beside her and the night that was separate from her life became her life, all of it, and all the other nights she had lived and would live belonged to another woman.

She woke and saw with a shock that the night was fading into grayness. There was a strange sound outside the cabin door. In a moment it was repeated and she realized an Indian was there, grunting as Indians usually did instead of knocking when they wanted to be admitted. She shook David and he woke and got his revolver and opened the door. She heard the Indian say in Chinook, "I come from Tilluk." Then David went outside and closed the door.

She got up. In a moment David and the Indian came into the cabin.

"This man is hungry," David said, motioning to the Indian to sit down. "I'll fix breakfast."

"I have to go," Ann said.

She waited till he got the fire going and water heating, then he walked part of the way with her. When they were in sight of the farm, he held her a moment and said, "You mustn't marry Holland."

"There's no use talking about it. I'm going to."

"Let the place go. Your father can start over. It will be hard on him, but he'll make out. When that road's done, the land will be quickly taken. Prices will go up . . ."

She was amazed to hear him talking just like her father. But she was disappointed, too, because he offered her nothing of himself. He had told her she didn't love Holland. Why didn't he tell her the rest of the truth—that she loved *him?* Apparently, he didn't want to face that.

She said, "I have to hurry, David."

"I'm going away for a while—maybe a week," he said. "I'll see you when I get back."

"David, it's over. It will never happen again." She said it as emphatically as she could and left him abruptly.

When she reached the kitchen, she could hear her father getting up. She built a fire in the stove and began to get breakfast. She must remember that she was in the hands of fate, she thought, and that things would work out as they were meant to work out. If she didn't hope for anything, she couldn't be disappointed. But how could a person keep from hoping?

That evening Holland brought the new mortgage, not due for a year. It was written in a precise hand, in awkward legal language. Ann and her father both read it carefully. Then Holland spoke.

"I'm a man slow to give my word and sure to keep it. I got it made out like I promised. But I didn't promise I'd sign it. I ain't a-goin' to till the day of our weddin'. There's no use arguin' or sweetin' up to me. I ain't a-goin' to."

13

THE INDIAN was a very small man with his head flattened and elongated grotesquely. He wore an ancient black sack coat aflutter with faded ribbons and bits of fur sewed on haphazardly. His sailcloth trousers were tucked into buckskin leggings dyed red. He made Dave think of a performing dog dressed up for a show.

During breakfast, he only grunted in reply to Dave's questions; but afterward he became talkative, sputtering long sentences in Chinook interspersed with English. He was a Klalam from Port Townsend and his name was Tseetsan, but white men called him Stephen. He had worked for many white men and prized a ragged packet of character testimonials. which he eagerly showed to Dave. Most were formal and meaningless, but one was revealing: *This will interjuce Stephen* [it read], *a Klalam who gided me Pt. Townsend to Olympia, spring of 51. Watch the sonabitch don't steal the buttons off your coat.*

He and his brother had got acquainted with Tilluk at Port Townsend. The man named Weller was there, living in a cabin a little way from town, and Tilluk and Stephen's brother were watching him. Stephen had come in a canoe paddled by six relatives, whom he had left at the place called Goglehitee or Commencement Bay. He had rented a horse there from a Puyallup chief, whom Dave owed a shirt in payment.

Dave packed a rucksack and they started out, racing their horses over fourteen miles of treacherous trail to the bay, reaching it in the middle of the morning. Dave paid the Puyallup for Stephen's horse, delighting him with a faded shirt, and left his own animal in care of DeLin, the sawmill owner.

Stephen led him to a section of beach where Puyallup squaws were putting salmon to smoke in little boxlike huts. The canoe was here but the crew was nowhere in sight and it took Stephen an hour to round them up. They were a tattered, dirty bunch, smelling of the fish oil with which they annointed their bodies—and of whisky. Since two were too drunk to be fit for anything but sleep, Stephen was for delaying the start; but Dave pointed out that he and Stephen could each take a paddle until the pair sobered up.

Paddling was hard work. The water was streaked with tidal currents and at one place near the mouth of the bay they got into a series of small whirlpools which spun and twisted the twenty-foot canoe and threatened to capsize it. It was a cool, overcast day, but in less than an hour Dave was drenched with sweat and his back ached. When the others stopped paddling, he was thankful for a moment's rest—then he saw they were passing a whisky bottle.

He demanded the bottle and they handed it to him, thinking he wanted to drink, but he set it between his feet and refused to let it make the rounds. The

Indians were offended. The man in front of him made a grab for the bottle, but Dave beat him to it and flung it over the gunwale. The crew stared in dismay and began to jabber angrily.

"I'll buy you another bottle when we reach Port Townsend," he said, but this seemed to make them feel more outraged than ever.

Stephen, sitting behind him, muttered, "Get out your revolver and cock it. They are talking about killing you."

Dave obeyed and the crew calmed down. However, they refused to work and the canoe drifted with the tide.

Stephen saved the day. He suddenly pointed to a bluff on an island to their left and began to chatter about it. The others were soon listening attentively and Dave gathered that he was telling a story about a battle that had been fought there many years ago. The Klalams were completely absorbed by the tale. When it was finished, they seemed to have forgotten their mutiny and they picked up their paddles and went to work. Stephen began a minor chant in time to the paddling and the others joined him. They were like children, Dave thought. He suddenly felt a warm affection for them and a new respect for Stephen.

They reached Elliot Bay that evening and beached near the mouth of the Duwamish River, midway between the settlements of New York Alki and Seattle. A band of Duwamish Indians were summering on the beach here, living in long houses of slabs and mats. The chief, a tall, stately man, came to meet

Dave and the Klalams, saying they were welcome to stay as long as they wished—provided they brought no whisky, which he would not allow among his people. His name was Sealth and he pronounced it for Dave with great care. The settlers at the head of the bay had named their town for him and he was somewhat upset because they were mispronouncing the name "Seattle."

Sealth invited Dave to spend the night in his lodge—a narrow, hundred-foot-long structure that was home for a dozen families. Dave lay on the mat floor, ate countless baked clams, and talked with Sealth until the chief fell asleep. Then, tired of the fishy-smoky air, he took his blanket and made his bed on the beach.

A fog had rolled in, dwindling the world to himself and a small patch of sand and stirring him with a vague excitement that kept him awake. He thought of Ann, missing her. For a while, he pretended that she was beside him and he indulged in a fantasy in which he convinced her that she mustn't marry Holland Gay. Then he called himself a skirt-struck dolt.

For her sake, he hoped she wouldn't marry Holland, but that didn't mean he wanted her himself. He didn't want to be tied to a woman. Or a claim. Or a family. He wanted to go back to Illinois and watch Ben Weller hang. And then he wanted his freedom. He wanted to work at whatever took his fancy and quit when he pleased and go where he pleased and spend his money as he pleased. This was what he had always wanted and so it must be what he still wanted.

He tried to think harshly of Ann, calling her a brainless girl who had thrown herself at him. He had no responsibility in the matter, no obligation to her. After a while, pretending she was beside him again, he fell asleep.

The bay was still smothered in fog the next morning. Dave was in favor of traveling anyway, but the Klalams refused to budge. "We will get lost," Stephen pointed out. "We will come out of the fog in a place we don't know and we will be lost and lose much time."

By noon, visibility was better and the Indians grumblingly shoved off. Wind and tide were both against them and they made poor time. In an hour it began to rain. All of the crew were sober and Dave didn't have to paddle but occasionally he relieved one of them just to keep warm. They traveled till dark, when they landed on Whidby Island. He was prepared for a miserable night, but they camped against the curving wall of a bluff where they were somewhat sheltered and which reflected the heat from a big fire and dried them out. They made huts of boughs and the Indians painstakingly dried quantities of ferns and grass to sleep on.

They got an early start the next morning, which was bright and crisp. The Sound was choppy, but shortly after noon they rounded Marrowstone Point and saw Port Townsend lying at the foot of a low, symmetrical plateau four miles away.

Dave was surprised at the apparent size of the town. Three large warehouses claimed the waterfront and behind them other buildings seemed to be massed in citylike solidarity. Three ships were anchored offshore—two brigs and a small but luxurious-looking stern-wheeler. Docks were large and piled with cargo. As they drew near, however, the illusion faded. Three quarters of the town consisted of Indian shacks.

A group of Indian children raced to meet the canoe as it rasped onto the pebbly beach. Dave went at once to a store and bought seven blankets as payment for his crew and a hunting knife as a bonus for Stephen. Reluctant to replace the whisky he had thrown overboard, he substituted a jug of blackstrap molasses, which was scarce and expensive and which Indians prized as a confection. The crew sat down on the beach and began to gulp it down, and he was sure they would all be sick. Stephen disliked leaving the party, but Dave insisted on being taken at once to Tilluk and they set out on a road that led eastward out of town through heavy timber.

He and his brother lived about a mile down the road, Stephen said, and Ben Weller's cabin was not far away. It was hidden deeply in the woods and he and his brother probably never would have found it if they hadn't helped build it. Weller had told them he would put a curse on them if they ever told its location; but if he had the gift of cursing, why did he have to hide from his enemies?

Stephen's cabin and his brother's stood close together beside the road, little slab huts that housed four plump squaws and half a dozen children. Tilluk was not there. Stephen conversed with his brother for a long time in their tribal tongue before speaking to Dave in Chinook.

"The man named Weller has gone," he said finally. "Tilluk has followed him. They left the night before last—the foggy night."

For a moment Dave let himself feel beaten. He went out of the hut and stood in the road, looking at nothing, letting frustration seethe in him. He was tired and hungry and his money was nearly gone. It seemed to him that perhaps Ben Weller had the power of cursing his enemies after all.

Stephen came out of the hut and handed him a piece of smoked venison wrapped in a cold pancake. "Eat something. You will feel better."

Dave bit into the unappetizing food, thinking it would very likely poison him and not much caring if it did.

"Does your brother know where they went?" he asked.

"Weller boarded a ship about to sail and Tilluk took work on the same ship. He had to promise to stay on the ship for a long voyage, but he said he would leave it when Weller did. From here the ship would go to Seattle, he said, and then to Olympia."

Dave groaned mentally, remembering a lumber brig that had slipped to the head of Elliot Bay the day before when the fog had thinned and they were getting ready to set out in the canoe. Very likely it was the ship Tilluk and Weller were on and had been lying off the bay in the fog. Heaven only knew where they would be by the time he could get back there.

He asked to be taken to Weller's cabin then, and

Stephen led him a little way along the road toward town, and turned around a bush into a trail Dave would never have found. They followed its twisted course among massive firs for perhaps a quarter of a mile; then Stephen stopped and pointed to his right. After a moment, Dave saw the shuttered window of a cabin twenty yards away, almost hidden by foliage.

The trail led straight on and they had to leave it and push through the brush to get to the cabin. The door was padlocked. The windows were closed by inswinging shutters, tightly barred. After trying vainly to force one of these, Dave borrowed Stephen's new knife, got the blade between the shutter and the casing and cut the leather hinges. The shutter fell away and he crawled in.

The small building was stocked with food and whisky and was a veritable arsenal. There were three loaded rifles, a big Colt revolver and a shotgun. The window Dave had opened faced the trail and offered a perfect opportunity to ambush anyone approaching the cabin.

Weller's cautious way of living was perfectly clear now. By traveling on lumber ships, living on them and confining his card-playing to them, he left no trail in any of the settlements. A law officer seeking a man of Bart Hadder's description would be likely to be soon discouraged. The cabin was an additional precaution. It was a hiding place, a refuge where he could do his solitary drinking, a trap to which he could lead a pursuer and quietly do away with him.

Looking over the cabin, Dave discovered that most of Weller's possessions were packed into a small chest and a carpetbag. He wondered if the man kept these packed as a matter of course—so as to be always ready for a sudden departure. Or had they been recently packed? The answer was provided by a copy of the Olympia *Columbian* wrapped around a pair of shoes. It was less than a week old, and Dave whistled. It looked as if Ben Weller was getting ready for a long journey—and soon.

In a mahogany glove box in the chest, Dave found several keys, one of which looked as if it was a duplicate to the padlock on the door. He climbed out through the window and found that it was. He then rummaged around until he found an old strap and hammer and nails, and he carefully replaced the hinges on the window.

He walked back to town and learned that the steamer was sailing up the Sound the next day, would put in at Seattle, and would take him as a passenger. This was really good luck, for it would get him there as soon as he could make it by canoe, even if he were able to round up a crew and leave at once.

He checked with the customs office and learned that the ship that had sailed the night before last was the brig *Mary Dare.* He got a meal and a room, bought a supply of cigars, and wrote a letter to the Governor of Illinois reporting in detail what he had learned about Hadder-Weller. *"This will give you something to go on,"* he wrote in conclusion, *"in the event of my death before my mission is completed.*"

Next, he wrote a long letter to Ann. It began rather formally, became very informal indeed, and ended up in scraps in a cuspidor. But he felt considerably better for having written it.

14

SALLY KNEW the symptoms and she was worried. Roy had been sober for nearly three months but now he was restless and irritable and she knew he often felt the need of a drink. These spells were to be expected, of course. Ordinarily, they wouldn't last more than a day or two; but now he was worried about some business matter that he was keeping to himself and that was increasing the tension on him day by day. It was a real test, she thought. If she could get him through it, she could begin to feel he had dried up for good.

She was the only person who understood that Roy mustn't drink anything, ever, and she was the only one who could make him understand it. It was lucky she'd come to Seattle when she did. Another year and he'd have drunk up everything he had.

Shortly after he'd gone back east, his father had died and left him property worth twelve thousand dollars—a small fortune in those times. He'd got out of the army and turned everything into cash with the idea of coming west and going into the lumber business. He was drinking heavily by that time and the money was going fast, but he had managed to buy a small sawmill which, in spite of having been neglected, now furnished them with a good living. Besides that, he still had around four thousand dollars in cash in a Portland bank, which he intended to invest in modern, steam-driven mill machinery.

Sally had found something like happiness here in this crude beginning of a town. She had a nicer home and more money to spend than she had ever hoped for. More important, Roy needed her and he knew it. She had no fear of his ever leaving her again. At the same time, she knew he hadn't changed basically— he was still occasionally embarrassed about having an Indian wife. But she believed they were getting over that hurdle too.

Most of the rougher, semi-literate settlers judged her solely by the color of her skin, she knew. To them she was a squaw and always would be. But better educated people, including some of Seattle's business and social leaders, were more likely to take her on her merits.

As long as she lived, she would never forget that first Sunday she and Roy had gone to church. Roy had been sober only two weeks, was still shaky, and didn't want to go. She didn't either, if the truth were known. They had to appear in public together sometime and she thought they might as well face up to it. She insisted and they went.

There was no preacher in Seattle yet and no church except a big unfinished warehouse that the group used temporarily. The service was conducted by a layman, who made no attempt at a sermon but merely read from the Bible and led the singing. She was the only Indian there, of course. She felt the stares of the others and she saw that Roy was miserable. When the service was over, they made no attempt to take part in the handshaking and chatting in front of the building but started at once for home. Then Arthur Denny, who was the most influential man in town, called to them. He and Mrs. Denny came over and welcomed them to the group and asked them to Sunday dinner. They had a delightful afternoon and Sally went home warmed by the discovery that there were churchgoers who did sometimes practice what they professed. Others took their cue from the Dennys and she never felt out of place in church again.

She and Roy became part of a small circle of young people who met once in a while for dinner parties, lent one another books, went on picnics. It was a conservative, rather staid group; but she was accepted completely and she was happy in it. And besides, there were Roy's business friends: sea captains, merchants—and Ben Weller.

Ben dropped in every two weeks or so, always asking for cedar or spruce or some other lumber Roy didn't have on hand. He would then invite Roy to a card game on board ship. Ben never drank when he was playing and this made it easier for Roy to abstain, too; so Sally didn't mind his playing, though he lost more often than he won.

It was something Ben had told Roy that was bothering him—she was pretty sure of that. It was after Ben had spent an afternoon at the mill that Roy had come home upset. He had refused to tell her what was wrong except to hint he was in danger of losing the mill. She didn't see how that could be, because he was the sole owner and not in debt. Since she couldn't get the facts out of him, she determined to get them out of Ben.

She got her opportunity one rainy afternoon when she was alone in the house and Ben dropped in unexpectedly, as he always did. She gave him her best smile, even let him flirt with her a little, and then asked him bluntly what Roy was troubled about. Ben was surprised that she didn't know. After a little insisting on her part, he told her.

"He's in pretty bad trouble and you certainly have a right to know about it," Ben said. "He's been cutting timber on government land. Fred Filler told me that they've got the goods on him and they're going to prosecute. Fred is a good friend of mine. He lives in Olympia and he's in with that land office crowd."

Sally was stunned. She knew Roy was guilty of cutting timber on land that belonged to the federal government—but so was practically every other mill owner on the Sound. In a country where there were a thousand acres of forest for every one of prairie, most people felt that every tree felled was an improvement—one more that some homesteader wouldn't have to cut or girdle.

"Why pick on Roy?" she said.

"Washington has decided to stop illegal cutting once and for all. They've chosen Roy to make an example of. They picked him because he had his loggers on salary instead of buying logs by the foot as most operators do. That makes him directly responsible for the logging and gives Uncle Sam an open-and-shut case."

"What will they do to him?"

"He stands to get a whopping fine—more than the mill is worth—and possibly even a jail sentence."

Sally tried to grasp this. Roy couldn't stand this kind of shock now. He'd go back on the bottle. Even if he didn't go to jail, it meant the end of him.

"I don't see how it can be such a serious thing," she said. "You can buy timberland for a dollar and a quarter an acre!"

"It's serious, believe me." Ben watched her tensely for a moment, then sat back in his chair. "However, I think I've found a way to get him out of trouble."

He refused to tell her his plan just then because he hadn't yet discussed it with Roy. However, he came to dinner that night and afterward he and Roy talked in the living room. Sally stayed in the kitchen, pretending to help the Duwamish woman she was teaching civilized cooking and the elementary rules of cleanliness. But mostly she listened to them talking over Ben's proposal.

"You've been cutting helter-skelter over three thousand acres," Ben said. "If you could buy that land and get the title back-dated, your troubles would be over. Fred Filler says that can be done if you'll grease a few palms."

"Sounds like I might get in deeper than ever," Roy said.

"The thing can be done safely enough through Filler. You won't have to contact anyone at the land office. In fact, it would be wise for you not to go near the place."

"How much will it cost me?"

"Thirty-seven hundred and fifty dollars for the land. Another five hundred for palm-grease."

Roy whistled through his teeth. "That's a lot of money."

It was, Sally knew, just about exactly the amount he had on deposit in Portland.

"Well, you'll have the land," Ben said. "A lot of people think timberland is bound to go up."

"I don't like bribing those rascals. I cut the damn timber and I don't know but what I'd rather throw myself on the mercy of the court."

"Roy, I tell you that U.S. district attorney is laying for you. He's under pressure from the Attorney General to make an example of you that will stop cutting on government land all over Washington and Oregon."

After a silence, Roy said, "Damn it, I can't think straight. I'd give anything if I could take a drink or two and stop."

Sally burst into the room, then.

"That's enough of that talk," she said cheerfully. "Yes—I know all about the whole thing. I got it out of Ben. And I know this—it's nothing compared to the mess you'll be in if you take that first drink."

Ben laughed at that and then Roy laughed too.

"She's wonderful," Ben said.

Sally curtsied demurely and they laughed again.

"Well, Mrs. Longnose," Roy chided, "what's your opinion? Shall I buy the land?"

She didn't see that there was anything else to do. She didn't know much about courts and lawyers, but she was pretty sure Roy couldn't stand the tension of a trial right now without drinking.

"I should think so, Roy—if that will settle it once and for all."

"I'm leaving for Olympia tonight on the *Mary Dare*," Ben said. "She'll be in port there a day and a half. That'll give me time to see Filler and get the title made out."

"All right," Roy said. "But tell him there'll be no money until the title is in my hands."

Ben frowned. "Well, he ought to agree to that. But he'll want the money on the line when it's delivered. He'll want it in gold."

"I'll have to go to Portland to get it. I'll leave tomorrow and meet him in Olympia in a week."

"You'd better stay out of Olympia," Ben said. "I'll bring Filler here. I'll have him here a week from tonight with the title signed and back-dated."

"That will be the sixteenth," Roy said.

Ben left shortly after that, not wanting to miss his ship. Roy went to the door with him and said, "Ben, let me know what your expenses are."

"Forget it," Ben said. "I'm in this just for the fun of it. Simply can't resist skulduggery."

Roy closed the door and came back into the room looking very solemn. "It isn't like Ben to refuse expense money. I wonder if he has a finger in the pie somewhere."

"I wouldn't think he was that kind," Sally said.
"You never played cards with him," Roy said.

Roy left early the next morning for Portland, traveling on horseback and taking a reliable man from the mill with him. The house suddenly seemed very big and empty to Sally and she fought a feeling of being a stranger in it. She tried to keep busy with housework and sewing and by teaching the Duwamish woman to bake a cake. She asked the woman to stay nights until Roy got back, and fixed her a bed in the kitchen.

Sally was not a woman given to foolish fears, but the feeling of strangeness persisted. It seemed as if she had never really lived in the house with Roy, as if their having been together here were a dream, as if he would never be here again. She told herself it was perfectly ridiculous to sit around thinking of all the things that could happen to him on the long trip over the Cowlitz trail; nevertheless, she caught herself doing it time and again.

The afternoon of the second day, a steamer whistled in the bay and Sally walked down to see it come in. It was a pleasant day with the sun bright and warm and a light breeze blowing in over the bay, and half the town had turned out to line the waterfront and watch the sight. The little stern-wheeler churned in slowly, slid expertly up to the dock, and tied up. The gangplank tipped down and half a dozen passengers disembarked, faintly self-conscious as the focal point of so large an audience.

The last one off was Dave, looking rather picturesque with his rucksack on his back, carbine in hand, and his low crowned black hat pushed back on his head. He paused on the dock to look over the crowd, and Sally had the feeling he was seeing everyone in it. He recognized her at once, grinned, and came over to her.

He asked how she was getting along and she told him about Roy and the mill and proudly pointed out her house. He seemed glad to see her, but from time to time he glanced around nervously. He seemed especially interested in a sailing ship that was loading lumber at the mill dock.

"I was hoping to meet an Indian here," he said. "He's working on the *Mary Dare.* Is that her?"

"The *Mary Dare*—that's the ship Ben sailed on. She sailed the night before last."

"Ben?"

"Ben Weller. He's sort of a business friend of ours."

Dave looked startled, then he sighed. "I've been chasing Ben Weller all over the Sound. Now I guess I'm on my way to Olympia."

"Business?"

He nodded. "Do you know if he'll be in Olympia long?"

Sally frowned, trying to remember. "I think he said a day and a half. Then I think he's going somewhere else before he comes back here. Victoria or somewhere."

"He's coming back here soon?"

"He and Roy have some business to do on the sixteenth. They'll be at our house. Shall I tell him you're looking for him?"

"No," Dave said, "I'd rather you didn't. It will be an advantage to catch him off guard."

Dave was studying her strangely. "How well do you know Weller?" he asked.

"As well as I know anyone here. Roy knows him better than I do. He's Roy's agent and now they're in—well, a timber deal together. Why?"

He looked at her intensely, as if he wanted to tell her something. Then he seemed to change his mind.

"He has a rotten reputation," he said guardedly. "If I were you, I wouldn't trust him too far. Tell your husband that."

Ben Weller lazed in his cabin all day while the *Mary Dare* unloaded a consignment of dry goods at the Olympia dock and took on smoked fish and lumber. He slept, read the *Columbian,* spent a lot of time practicing with a deck of cards, dealing from the bottom so skillfully that a witness would have sworn the cards came from the top. He had supper with the ship's officers and got up a poker game that broke up before midnight. Then he went ashore.

He visited several saloons, drinking buttermilk. In one of these he discovered the wizened little man he knew to be the town watchman, who guarded the business district against burglary. The man sat in a dark corner against the wall and his eyes closed. At five minutes to twelve he got to his feet and went out. Ben watched him walk the length of the street, trying every door. In a quarter of an hour he was back in his chair.

Ben spent the next two hours on the ship; then, when the streets were deserted except for a staggering drunk or two, he came ashore again. Two saloons were still open and the sallow haze of their windows was the only light on the muddy, curving business street. The watchman zigzagged from door to door. Ben stood close to the black hulk of a building until the man finished his rounds and went into the saloon.

Ben moved swiftly to the land office, feeling himself a part of the darkness. He paused before the padlocked door and looked back down the street. He thought he saw a movement in the darkness behind him and he moved on, ducking into a narrow space between two buildings. When he had waited several minutes without seeing a further sign of life, he went back to the land office.

He took a short piece of watchspring from his pocket, pushed it into the lock beside the bow, pushed back the spring catch, and removed the lock as easily as he would pick a plum. He shoved the door open quietly, and went in. In the shielded light of matches, he found his way to a cabinet and searched the drawers until he found a supply of blank title forms. He folded several of these, slipped them into his pocket and left, carefully padlocking the door again.

The next day the *Mary Dare* sailed a hundred miles north to a little settlement called Whatcom; then she put in briefly at Victoria, in British territory, before heading through the strait to the ocean. Ben left her at the latter port and hired a canoe manned by Nook Lummi Indians to take him across thirty-five miles of rough water to Port Townsend. There he ascertained that the bark *Blue Gull* would sail the next day for Seattle; then he walked to his cabin in the woods.

Working by lamplight, using ink of the exact shade used by the Olympia land office, he wrote out a title to three thousand acres of timberland near Elliot Bay. With a slightly different ink he reproduced the signature of the land commissioner. Laying the paper over a fifty-dollar gold coin and rubbing with the blunt end of the pen, he produced an indistinct but plausible seal.

15

IT WAS EARLY afternoon when Dave left Sally at the dock. He found a blacksmith who had a horse to rent, which he promised to return by the sixteenth. He made a thirty-mile ride over Indian trails to Commencement Bay, got his own horse from DeLin, and reached the Covey clearing well after dark. There was a light in the kitchen and he was unable to suppress a feeling of excitement at the prospect of seeing Ann.

But as he rode toward the window at a walk, his heart sank. Ann and Holland Gay stood together near the window, kissing, stepping apart when they heard the sound of hoofs. Ann came to the back door.

"You're back," she said in a tone which might have conveyed either relief or annoyance.

"I guess you're busy," he said, not getting off his horse.

"Holland's here."

"I saw him. Through the window."

"David, did you find—Uncle Ben?"

"No."

There was nothing to say for a moment and they studied each other, without self-consciousness at first—then he gave her a smile she didn't return.

"Are you going to come in?"

"I'll see you later." He looked her in the eye, trying to give a special meaning to the words.

"Tomorrow?"

"Tonight."

She surely understood then, but she said blandly, "I'm going to bed right away. I was just telling Holland good night."

Holland came to the doorway behind her and slipped his hands around her waist and folded them.

Dave rode to his cabin infuriated with her. He had never thought much about her kissing Holland, supposing she did it dutifully and without passion. If she comes to me tonight, I won't touch her, he thought. I'll tell her I don't want her in my arms after she's been in his. He knew there was little truth in this, but the thought was bitterly consoling.

He had got a fire going and was fixing a meal when he heard a grunt at the cabin door and found Tilluk there, footsore and exhausted.

"The work of following the man called Weller has gone very badly," Tilluk said. "I sent for you at Port Townsend but he left on a ship. I took work on the same ship. I know nothing about a ship and don't understand English well and it was very bad. I was beaten by the *tyee* of the crew, the mate. In Olympia I learned that the ship would sail north into the country of the Haidas and the other fierce tribes that hate my people. After that it would go to a faraway place called California. I was afraid to go to the north country or to California. This morning I left the ship."

"You did right," Dave said. He explained that he

had been to Port Townsend with Stephen but had been too late.

Tilluk brightened. "Perhaps my work has been worth a blanket after all."

Dave laughed. A two-and-a-half-point blanket cost three dollars. "You come into Steilacoom with me. You can have blankets and shirts and anything else that pleases your eye."

Tilluk joined him in a meal of bacon and pancakes and then left to see his relatives.

Dave sat on his doorstep a while, smoking, looking into the black shadows of his meadow. The long trip had been tiring and frustrating; yet he at last had advance knowledge of Ben Weller's movements. Unless his luck was very bad, he would catch up with Weller in Seattle on the sixteenth. He would play it safe, he decided. He wouldn't try to take the big man alone but would ask Captain Maloney to detail a soldier to go with him.

He went to bed thinking of Ann, hoping she would come to him again and knowing she wouldn't. He dreamed she knocked on the door but he couldn't wake to open it. He wrenched awake and saw that the door was partly open. He lay still, staring into the dark corner of the cabin behind the door, seeing something move there.

"Ann?" he said. A shadow moved toward him and took shape.

"Hello, Boston."

He knew the ugly, arrogant voice at once.

"Hello, Suchamuch."

The Indian had him covered with a double-barreled rifle. His bed was against the end of the cabin and parallel to it and he lay with his left side to the wall. His gunbelt hung above the bed from a peg in the wall. Getting his revolver meant sitting up and reaching across himself. There was no chance of getting it in time.

"I kill you now, Boston."

"Why?" he said, stalling, trying to think. "I could have killed you that day on the dock. I didn't."

Suchamuch grunted. "I kill you because you are a Boston. The Bostons take the land, drive the game away, pay the Indian nothing to work and make them rich. The Bostons will destroy the Indian and this will be their country. But it will not be your country, Boston. You are one Boston who will die."

There's nothing to do but reach for the revolver, Dave thought. I'll move fast and perhaps he'll miss in the dark or hit me in a place that isn't vital. It's a very small chance because he has a double-barreled rifle. And if he's loaded with buckshot, I'm as good as dead. Then he saw another shadow behind Suchamuch, a squat figure that slid through the partly open doorway and raised a weapon.

"Captain Maloney will know who killed me," Dave said. "You will hang."

"Captain Maloney believe I have gone over the mountains with my people," Suchamuch sneered.

They were his last words. The axe blade crushed deep into his brain. He grunted and collapsed on the floor.

"I have killed him," Tilluk said.

Dave lighted a lamp and saw the mess of blood and whitish brains and felt sick.

"He was at the camp of the Puyallups," Tilluk said. "He was drinking whisky and he talked with great hatred for you. He asked some of the men to come with him and kill you, but their hearts were good and they would not do it. He came alone and I followed him. I am sick that I killed him. I will hang."

"I promise that you won't hang," Dave said.

"I will run away. I will go on a ship to California."

"No. Killing him was the only way you could stop him from killing me, so you did right to kill him. The law is fair. We'll go to Captain Maloney, who knows that Suchamuch was a bad man. He'll tell us what to do."

"We could bury Suchamuch. No one would know."

"The Puyallups would know. The news would get to Steilacoom. It's better for you to face the law now and be cleared. Then you won't have to live in fear."

Tilluk thought this over, patently doubtful. Finally, he said, "I will do whatever you say."

They rode to Fort Steilacoom with Suchamuch's body wrapped in a tarpaulin and slung over a shaggy Puyallup pony Tilluk borrowed from one of his relatives. Dave told Captain Maloney what had happened. Then the three of them rode into town to the big frame courthouse and he told the story again to the prosecuting attorney and the sheriff, who had recovered from his illness and was back on duty. Then all except Maloney made the long trip back to the claim to look at the scene of the killing.

While there, the prosecuting attorney questioned Tilluk in great detail in Chinook and brought out a revealing bit of information. At the Puyallup camp, Suchamuch had promised rewards to several men in an effort to get them to come with him to kill Dave. He knew a white man, he had said, who would pay many blankets for Dave's death.

"Who would that be?" the attorney asked.

"I don't know," Dave said.

In all probability, it was Holland Gay. Holland had seen him fight Suchamuch, had heard Suchamuch threaten him, and knew the Indian could easily be enticed into killing him. Probably the attorney suspected Holland, too, since Dave's feud with him was common knowledge. But Dave was afraid that to bring another person into the affair would complicate matters and drag out the business of getting Tilluk clear. Apparently the attorney felt the same way.

"Well, I'm satisfied," he said. "How about you, Sheriff?"

"I think Tilluk ought to have a medal," John Bradley, the sheriff, said.

"Now here's what we'll do," the attorney said. "We'll bring the boy before a grand jury. His action was clearly justifiable and he won't be indicted. I'll guarantee it."

"Can't you just refuse to arrest him?" Dave said.

"It will be better to have a jury give him his

freedom. Even though it will be cut and dried, it will be an action of the citizens. That will be better for the boy."

The plan went through without a hitch but with a considerable amount of delay and it consumed all of Dave's time for the next three days. On the afternoon of the fourteenth, Tilluk was exonerated.

He and Dave found themselves something like popular heros. Half the town came to the big frame courthouse to congratulate them. Captain Maloney had come down from the fort accompanied by a straight-backed lieutenant named Phil Sheridan, just out of West Point. They made a little show of shaking hands with Tilluk.

"You did a good thing by coming to the authorities instead of trying to cover up the killing," Maloney said, speaking in Chinook and making sure that his voice carried to the Puyallup and Nisqually chiefs who were there. "You've shown the Indian that, while our law is stern, it is also just and he can trust it."

When he got a chance, Dave called Maloney aside. He had already told the captain that he expected to find Weller in Seattle on the sixteenth. He now said that he planned to leave early the next morning so as to arrive about noon—a day before Weller was due to meet Sally's husband. Maloney agreed to send a sergeant along with him and they arranged a meeting place near Dave's cabin.

"If there's a local peace officer in Seattle, let him make the arrest," Maloney said. "The sergeant can be present, of course; but, technically, he's going along merely to bring the prisoner back to Fort Steilacoom.''

Dave and Tilluk walked down the steep grade to Commercial Street. Before getting their horses at the livery, they stopped at Balch's to leave word that the rights to Dave's claim were for sale. Dave hated to do it, but the time had come. He would need the money to get back to Illinois for the hanging.

Balch was surprised. "You leaving the country?"

Dave said he was.

"I think you're foolish," Balch said. "There should be no difficulty in getting a little cash for that clearing, but you'll get very little compared to what it will be worth in a few years."

"I expect you're right. But I can't wait."

"Why not? You've got a future here. Folks like you. You got yourself a little notoriety as a fighter, but most people are sympathetic too—In this country, it's a good thing to be able to fight if you have to. And this business you've just been through has helped your reputation. You went to a lot of trouble to get your Indian free and the town respects you for it."

Dave laughed, pleased and embarrassed. "I appreciate your saying that, but it doesn't change anything."

"When the new governor gets here, there'll be an election," Balch said. "You could run for office and win. You could have a seat in the legislature if you want it."

"Me?" Dave said. "I never thought of anything like that."

"You're better qualified than most. I'd be glad to stump for you."

A fat, pale man came into the store and came up to Dave.

"You Dave Porter? . . . There's a soldier wants to see you. Captain Maloney."

"I just left him," Dave said. "What does he want?"

"I wouldn't know that. He's in Gay's saloon argufyin' with Gay about somethin'. He sent me for you."

16

HOLLAND GAY sat at a table in his saloon dealing solitaire and keeping an eye on a very drunk man at the bar. The man was very nearly out of money and on the verge of trying to mooch drinks. When that happened, Holland would nod at the bartender and the man would find himself on the seat of his pants in the street.

Holland had just heard the news that Tilluk was free. He was greatly relieved to know that the matter was settled without his being brought into it. It would have been like Dave Porter to twist things around so it looked as if Holland had hired Suchamuch to kill him. That would have been a dirty lie. He'd merely told the Injun where Dave could be found and had given him a rifle and a bottle of whisky. It was none of his affair if the Injun hated Dave and wanted to kill him.

He moved the cards automatically, missing many plays, and lapsed into a stream of brooding thoughts. His competitors were telling lies about him, giving his place a bad name; his bartenders were cheating him; the man who ran his Fox Island still was selling whisky on his own. Even Ann had taken advantage of him, making him get that new mortgage ready. He'd probably have to sign it, too, before the pretty little schemer would marry him.

He enjoyed this listing of grudges and found inspiration in it. If you cherished a grudge long enough, you thought of a way to get even. And the thoughts that came to him were petty or vicious without bothering his conscience in the least. In fact, he would feel uncomfortable if he thought the cheaters were going to get off without retribution. Cheaters deserved to be cheated.

A bearded man wearing the cap of a ship's officer came into the saloon, spoke to the bartender, and came over to Holland's table. Holland nodded him to a chair, knowing what he wanted.

"You off the *Amy Lester*?" Holland asked.

The man nodded. "I'm mate on her."

"She ready to sail?"

"Not till we get more of a crew. They been jumpin' ship like frogs offen a hot stove."

"How many you need?"

"Anyways three. More if we can get 'em."

Holland studied the drunk at the bar. He was trying to mooch a drink from two loggers who had just come in.

"I'll have one," Holland said. "What you payin'?"

"Twenty for whites, ten for Injuns."

Holland caught the bartender's eye and nodded at the drunk, then at the man across the table. The bartender called the drunk to the end of the bar and set up a drink.

"We'll pick him up in half an hour," the mate said.

"He'll be ready."

The bartender had left the bottle on the bar and the

drunk was helping himself. The two loggers were watching with amusement. They might catch on to what was happening, but Holland didn't much care. He was going to make twenty dollars just like finding it. Besides, he was going to sell the saloon just as soon as he could. Folks looked down on a saloon-keeper. He was going to marry and settle down and get into something more respectable.

He got up and followed the mate to the door and watched him go into another saloon. There wouldn't be anything there, he thought—not at this time of day. A block and a half away, Dave Porter and his Injun came down Balch Street and crossed Commercial, headed for Balch's store. Holland cleared his throat and spat.

That Dave Porter was lucky, just lucky. He should be dead and buried with his head blown off and his land open to claim. He was a bad one. A dirty fighter and a claim jumper. The people of Steilacoom oughtn't to put up with trash like that. But Dave had twisted things around and made Holland look like the claim jumper and himself like an honest man. And now folks were speaking highly of him because he'd gone to such pains to get his Injun cleared of a dirty killing.

Holland watched the pair go into the store and stood looking at the building after they had disappeared. He was smarter than Dave Porter, he thought. He'd proved it by getting Ann away from him. And, one way or another, he would get that claim too. Eventually, he would have Covey's six hundred and forty acres, even if he had to wait for Ike to die, and Dave's claim would make almost a thousand acres in a piece. All he had to do was get rid of Dave. And then a delightful idea came to him and he giggled inwardly.

He turned back into the saloon, jerked his head at the bartender, and went into the back room. The bartender followed him and closed the door.

"Dave Porter is down to Balch's," Holland said. "You go down there and tell him to come here. Tell him Captain Maloney is here and wants him. Tell him the captain and me is havin' a argument—that ought to sound convincin'."

The bartender's pouchy little eyes showed a flicker of doubt. "We ain't goin' to give him the business? Not him?"

"You do like I say. You got to hurry."

The bartender threw his apron on a chair and went out the back door. Holland went out to the bar and served the customers, then returned to the back room. He left the door open a crack and watched through it for several minutes. Finally, Dave and the bartender came into the saloon. Holland stepped back and took a place at the table.

The bartender pushed open the door, standing aside for Dave. Dave came in and looked around suspiciously.

"Where's the captain?" Dave said.

"He'll be right back," Holland said. "Have a chair."

Dave pulled out a chair and sat down.

"Bill," Holland said to the bartender. "Hand me that there account book."

The bartender moved to a shelf behind Dave and got the book. It was a maneuver they had used before and Bill understood perfectly what was expected of him. Holland opened the book, pretended to find a place in it, and extended it toward Dave with his finger pointing to one of the pages.

"Look at that," Holland said.

Puzzled, Dave bent forward to look. With a short chopping motion, the bartender laid a shot-loaded punch expertly across Dave's skull and he pitched forward on the table.

Holland got up and took off Dave's gunbelt and took the blackjack from the bartender.

"Go tend to the customers," Holland said. "Then bring in the other one."

Tilluk, waited in front of Balch's for a few minutes. He was overjoyed at being free and anxious to get back to his people and it was hard to stand still and wait. He idled up the street to Gay's saloon, looked in and was surprised to see that Dave was not there. He walked around the building to a winding alley lined with outhouses, chicken coops, woodpiles. The back door of the saloon was closed. There was a small window, but it was covered with a cloth and he couldn't see in. He could hear someone moving around in the back room, but he heard no voices.

Perplexed, he walked down the alley in the direction of Balch's. A cart rattled into the alley above him, pushed by two men. It was the type of cart used by ships' cooks to take supplies aboard. It stopped in back of Gay's.

Tilluk stepped behind a building and peered around the corner. The two men went into Gay's and in a moment came out with a sagging body between them and swung it into the cart. They immediately went in again and came out with another body, which Tilluk saw was Dave. They then arranged a tarpaulin over their load and pushed the cart back up the alley.

It had all happened so swiftly that Tilluk couldn't make any sense out of it. His first thought was that Dave was dead. He walked between buildings to the street and saw the cart headed for the dock south of town. He followed it at a distance and saw it pushed up the gangplank of a ship. Remembering stories he had heard about men being shanghaied, he at last grasped the truth. He thought of going to the fort and telling Captain Maloney, but he was afraid there wasn't time. The ship would sail.

He walked slowly onto the dock and up the gangplank, dreading what he had to do. A seaman met him on deck, greeted him in rough words he didn't understand.

Tilluk struggled with his meager English. "I —work." He waved his hand to indicate the ship.

"You want to work on the *Amy Lester?* You want to sail on her?" the seaman said.

"Yes."

"You crazy?"

"Yes," Tilluk said, not understanding.

The seaman laughed. "Come on. I'll take you to the mate."

* * *

In the back room of his saloon, Holland Gay pocketed the two double eagles the mate of the *Amy Lester* had left on the table. Then he examined the pile of papers and money that he had taken from the pockets of Dave and the drunk. Dave had had about twenty dollars in his pocket; the drunk, sixty cents. Holland made a neat stack of the coins and regarded them. Dave owed him twenty dollars and a good deal more for the cabin Nippin had built and the work he had done on the claim. He pocketed Dave's money, leaving sixty cents on the table. The drunk owed him at least sixty cents for the whisky, he thought, and so he pocketed that too.

He gave his attention to the papers, which had been in Dave's pocket. He unfolded one, blinked at it, and after a time realized it was a list of Chinook words. The other papers were letters. He read the first haltingly, not thinking it important till he saw it was signed by the Governor of Illinois. He studied them both a long time, becoming more and more disturbed. His hand was shaking when he folded them and slipped them into his hip pocket.

There was nothing specifically frightening about the letters, but they had set Holland to thinking. It was a shock to know that Dave Porter (or Partrey or whatever his name was) had semi-official status that was almost certainly known to Captain Maloney. It occurred to Holland for the first time that an effort might be made to trace Dave. For once, he wondered if he had made a mistake.

17

AT THE FIRST flickerings of consciousness, Dave was a mind without a body, an unstable awareness that confused itself with the sensations that came to it. And so he was pain, thirst, weakness. He was disaster and anger. He was a rough plank floor, the sound of heavy breathing, the reek of vomited alcohol. Then, slowly, he associated these things with his body and became a man again.

He made no effort to think back at first. After a long time, he pushed himself to a sitting position and was overwhelmed by a pain in his head and a sinking weakness. He wove in and out of consciousness again, touched something soft and realized with a shock that it was another human being.

They were in some sort of dark cubbyhole. He sat against a wall and the other man was sprawled on his back, breathing heavily. Dave had a splitting headache and one of his arms was numb. Something pressed uncomfortably against his back, and he discovered it was a timber with a trough cut into it, a waterway that ran along the floor against the wall. It was then he realized he was deep in the guts of a ship.

The room or locker or whatever it was was perhaps five feet by seven. It was almost pitch-dark and unbearably stuffy, the only ventilation coming from the small holes in the walls where the waterway passed under them. He stood up unsteadily. Stepping over the man on the floor and feeling his way along the walls, he found a low narrow door which seemed to be locked on the outside with a padlock.

There was nothing in the room but the other man and an empty bucket. Dave bent over the man and saw that he was middle-aged, bearded, and had vomited all over himself. Dave tried to bring him to by rubbing his palms. The man groaned and moved, but that was all.

Dave sank down against the wall again; he was frantically thirsty and his head was shrieking. Finally he slept. He was awakened by someone unlocking the door.

A big man with a curly blond beard looked in. He held a club in his hand.

"How about some drinking water?" Dave said.

"Well now," the man said. "One is awake."

He came into the room and stood with his club ready. "I'm third mate. You goin' to give us trouble?"

"I'm going to give you plenty," Dave said, "when I get off this tub."

The officer replied contemptuously and obscenely. He stood over Dave while two sailors brought in another unconscious man and laid him on the floor. The three left immediately but in a few minutes the officer returned and set a jug of water inside the door without saying a word.

The water was cool and fresh and Dave drank deeply. He bathed the faces of the other two men and brought one back to consciousness. The other seemed to be doped and there was no reviving him. The first was saturated with alcohol and was helplessly sick.

The stench was overpowering. Dave lay on his stomach with his nose near one of the holes in the wall where the air was better. After a while he slept again, and woke to find the ship under way. He had no idea how long he had been on the ship, but it seemed to him that the light was better and he thought a night must have passed.

The lock rattled and the door opened. A man in a cook's apron came in with a whisky bottle full of soup. Two sailors with billy clubs in their hands stood outside the door. Dave drank some of the soup, which was greasy and hardly warm. He passed the bottle to the sick man, who drank a swallow or two.

"Where we bound for?" Dave asked the man who had brought the soup.

"We'll put in at Seattle and Vancouver, then it's the Sandwich Islands."

Dave swore and the cook laughed at him. "You're in for a long voyage, lad, and I'll give you a piece of advice. Go along with your luck—don't buck it."

"I've got to see the captain."

The cook laughed again. "You can be sure they always wants to see the captain. It ain't allowed, lad."

"I'm no sailor. I've never worked on a ship," Dave protested inanely.

"That's plain to see."

"Somebody's going to pay for this."

"Well, supposin' you're right. Supposin' you

could go to the captain and convince him he made a mistake to take you on and you can make trouble for him. What would happen? Why, you'd be buried at sea, that's what. He'd see to it."

Dave saw the harsh truth of this and was smothered with a new sense of hopelessness. "When do we get out of this hole?"

"Maybe three days. Soon's we're out of the Sound."

"Three days! A man could die in here in three days."

"That he could, lad. I've seen 'em do it."

In an hour the ship dropped anchor and Dave knew they must be at Seattle. He gave way to his frustration then and got up and tried to rattle the door and slammed his body against it like a maniac. Both the other men were conscious now and the useless effort seemed to irritate them.

"Quiet down," one of them grumbled, "or you'll have that third mate in here a-swingin' a billy."

Dave sat down again, thinking he had never been so completely miserable in his life. He made himself sit perfectly quiet and tried to take a philosophical view of his luck.

I don't make the plans, he thought, *and there's no use stewing because I don't like them. If I get even a slight chance to get out of here, I'll take it. Whether I get it and whether I'm successful or not is up to the Planner.*

The thought calmed him and made it easier for him to pass the awful day in quiet. Perhaps death was like this, he thought, a black confinement from which you looked back on your life and longed for it and could do nothing about the longing. But it was not so much as this. It was the unconsciousness he had come out of, a greater blackness without wants or memories. It was nothing. And yet it seemed to him that if he were dead now his life itself would be left. All his conscious moments and his dreams, all he had done and thought—all this would not be dead. It was past but not gone. His immediate perception of it was gone and if he were dead his memory of it would be gone but it itself would always exist, discernible to some timeless consciousness. And there in the reeking darkness with the world shut out he saw this clearly and saw his life clearly and saw it as an angry, ugly thing.

The other men grew restless and talkative now, but he paid little attention to them. His head was much better and he was ravenously hungry. At last the door opened and a man came in with another bottle of soup. Dave took it and raised it to his lips to drink and saw with amazement that the man was Tilluk.

"They have me working in the kitchen," Tilluk said quietly in Chinook. "Can you swim?"

"Yes." Dave saw that two men guarded the door with clubs.

"I will try to steal the key and let you out, but we are anchored offshore and we will have to swim."

"Come as soon as you can."

While the other prisoners were drinking from the

bottle, Tilluk produced a sandwich from his shirt pocket and handed it to Dave. "I stole this. It isn't much but it will give you strength."

"What day is this?" Dave asked, his mouth full.

"You have been on the ship two nights," Tilluk said. "It is now the morning of the second day."

That would make today the sixteenth, Dave thought.

"Tilluk," he said, "how soon can you steal that key?"

"I don't know. It won't be easy to steal it."

"I hope I can get off the ship here, at Seattle," Dave said. "If I can't, you leave alone. The ship is going on a long voyage."

"I will stay until you're free."

"No. Get off here. Go to Captain Maloney and tell him the name of the ship. Tell him I was shanghaied by Holland Gay." He added, "And tell Ann Covey."

Tilluk nodded. He went out and one of the guards closed and locked the door.

Neither of the other prisoners had understood the conversation. Dave explained that Tilluk was going to steal the key and let them out. The men, both of whom had been to sea before, scoffed at the idea.

"Count me out," one of them said. "They'd put out a boat and meet us on the beach. Either that or pick us off with rifles before we'd swum twenty strokes."

"I can't swim, anyways," the other said.

Dave made himself wait calmly. He couldn't sleep and there was nothing to do but sit uncomfortably. After several hours, the other men began to express doubts that Tilluk would ever be back. Dave tried to reply good-naturedly. He pulled off his boots so as to be ready to swim. He kept telling himself that, with luck, he would still get ashore before Ben Weller left Seattle; but he was beginning to have his own doubts. Perhaps Tilluk had tried to steal the key and got caught. Perhaps he was in irons. Perhaps he had given up and deserted the ship.

It was a sickening shock to hear the grinding of the anchor chain on the capstan. Then the ship was in motion again, tipping slightly as the wind caught the sails, and the other prisoners laughed.

"You're lucky," one said. "You never would have made it."

"Hooray for the Sandwich Islands!" the other said.

He was answered by a crash just outside the door. The door flew open and Tilluk faced them with a hammer in his hand.

"I couldn't steal the key," he said apologetically, dropping the broken padlock to the deck. "So I stole a hammer."

Dave followed him through a disorder of rigging, sails, uncoiled hawsers, barrels, and crates. They reached a hatchway and climbed to the main deck, which was deserted, then on to the upper deck. It was a clear day at sunset. After two days in the dark, Dave was nearly blinded by the soft sunlight as he came through the hatchway. He had to close his eyes and do his looking in glimpses.

All hands were on deck. Tilluk darted to the rail,

climbed it, and gave a long piercing yell. A fool thing to do, Dave thought—it attracted the attention of every man on the ship. Dave was close behind him and as he swung a leg over the rail a seaman made a halfhearted attempt to grab him. Someone roared "Hold him! Hold him!" He hit the man a backhanded blow that backed him off and gave him time to jump.

In the quick look that he had before he left the rail, he saw the south shore of Elliot Bay an appalling distance away, saw the flats at the mouth of the Duwamish with half a dozen canoes trolling off them. They would be swimming against the current from the river—against the tide, too, for all he knew.

The shock of the icy water was paralyzing. He lost some of the air from his lungs. He thought he would never stop sinking. He worked his arms but was seized by the panicky thought that he had turned head downward and was trying to swim toward the bottom. He relaxed and at last broke the surface.

The water was not rough, but there was enough of a swell so that he was unable to locate Tilluk. In a moment, the Indian turned up at his side.

"It will be a long swim," Tilluk said.

Too long, Dave thought. He had done most of his swimming in Illinois rivers and waterholes; he had no idea how far he could swim. He was weak and stiff from his imprisonment and his muscles were already protesting against the exercise and the frigid water.

He rolled over on his back to look at the ship. It was farther away than he had expected but it had dropped anchor. Men were in the rigging furling sails. *They'll put out a boat,* he thought, *and overtake us long before we reach shore. Maybe it's for the best, at that. I'm not at all sure I can make shore.*

Tilluk raised himself in the water and gave the strange yell again and raised a hand and waved. Dave was startled; then he realized that Tilluk was trying to get the attention of the canoes fishing off the river mouth. It was their one hope. Dave raised himself, too, and could see them—black shapes in the pink sunlight. It seemed to him that one was fairly near—perhaps three times as far away as the ship. They changed their course and swam toward it.

He had to rest and turned over on his back again and saw a boat coming around the stern of the ship, a man standing in the bow with a rifle. Apparently he didn't sight them at once, for the boat headed almost straight astern of the ship. Dave rolled over and began to swim again. The next time he looked, the boat was coming directly for them. Tilluk was a better swimmer than he but kept with him. Dave stepped up his stroke but knew he couldn't keep it up long.

All at once the big faded-red canoe slid up, passed and reversed its direction before picking them up. He clung to its shell-studded gunwale while they pulled Tilluk in at the stern. Then strong arms hoisted him out of the water and sprawled him into the canoe.

The Indians were immediately paddling furiously and he knew the ship's boat must be very close. He was too exhausted to move for a moment, then he sat up and saw it, saw the man in the bow aiming a rifle.

He shouted a warning, somehow finding the right Chinook words, and the Indians bent low. The bullet whistled harmlessly overhead.

They reached shore well ahead of the boat. A group of Duwamish came down the beach from their huts to meet them and Dave recognized old Chief Sealth. He seized the dignified old Indian's hand and squeezed it warmly. It was a moment before Sealth remembered him. Then Dave quickly gave an account of what had happened.

Sealth smiled sadly and said something in a calm tone that sent his tribesmen running up the beach to their long, low houses. As the boat beached, the Duwamish streamed back—armed to the teeth with guns, knives, pogamoggans.

Sealth advanced to meet the boat and spoke briefly with the man in charge, who Dave assumed was the mate. In a moment Sealth came back with the men from the boat close behind him.

"He doesn't speak Chinook," Sealth said to Dave. "Tell him my people will not let him take you or the Puyallup. Tell him my people love peace and they do not like to interfere in the affairs of the white men, but if he tries to take you they will kill him."

Before the chief finished speaking, the mate halted in front of Dave and aimed his rifle at Dave's chest. "Get in the boat!" he snapped.

There were six men with the mate. The Indians surged around them, pressing them into a tight knot, jostling them against one another and against the mate.

"If you want to live a little longer," Dave said to the mate, "point that rifle at the ground."

The man hesitated, looking around him, fear showing in his eyes. He lowered the gun. Dave stepped up and gently took it from his hands. Someone slashed a handful of sand into the mate's eyes and he doubled up with his hands to his face. Two Indians pushed him backwards and tripped him and he sat down on the beach.

"Go back to your ship," Dave said. "I'll keep your rifle. I'm going to need it."

The mate got up and turned back to the boat without a word. His crew followed him eagerly, and they quickly shoved off.

Dave and Tilluk went with Sealth to his long slab house and stripped off their wet clothing.

"Will the *tyee* of the ship, the captain, make trouble for my people?" Sealth asked soberly.

"Don't worry," Dave said. "He won't try. He would only make trouble for himself."

Sealth shook his head doubtfully. "We do not grasp the white man's ways or his laws. If the *tyee* of the ship knows this, he might come back and make trouble. If so, I will call on you for help. Tell me where I can find you."

Dave moved one of the reed mats on the floor and drew a map on the sandy ground, showing the location of his claim. He said, "If I'm not there, go to Captain Maloney at Fort Steilacoom. I will tell him what happened and he will help you. There is nothing to worry about."

They traded their wet clothes for dry—ill-fitting trousers, flannel shirts, moccasins. Sealth gave Dave powder and ball and caps for the rifle he had taken from the mate. Dave was stiff and weak from his cramped imprisonment and chilled to the bone from his icy swim. Delay galled him, but a brief rest was a necessity. He and Tilluk warmed themselves at Sealth's fire and ate bread and smoked salmon washed down with hot clam juice. It was dark when they started on foot along the shore toward Seattle.

18

ROY GOT BACK from Portland on the afternoon of the sixteenth. Sally saw him coming up the skid road, riding beside Dock Jones, the man from his mill who had made the trip with him. She went out on the porch to meet them and, while they were still a hundred yards away, she could see Roy was so drunk he couldn't hit the ground with his hat.

He climbed down from his horse slowly and unsteadily and the three of them went into the house. Dock Jones brought in the saddlebags with the money in them and passed them to Sally.

"I tried to keep him dry," Dock said, "but he bought a quart in Portland. Never touched it till last night. Drank all night and bought another quart in Steilacoom this morning."

Dock left then, eager to see his family. Roy went upstairs to their bedroom. He took his rucksack with him, and Sally knew the bottle was in it. She followed him. He sat down on the bed and began to rummage around in the rucksack. Sally stashed the saddlebags away in the bottom drawer of a bureau.

"You know I'm drinking, don't you?" Roy demanded, speaking very deliberately in an effort not to slur his words. His eyes were glassy and defiant.

"I don't know what to do when you're at this

stage," Sally said. "If I take the bottle away from you, you'll get another or drink in a saloon. You can't get off the stuff until you're sick and dirty and unable to walk. Until it's sober up or die. Then, with my help, you can do it."

"Disgusted, aren't you?" He seemed heartily amused.

"Yes, just as I'd be disgusted if you were sick. I'd be disgusted with the sickness—not with you."

"You're disgusted with me," he asserted.

She tried another approach. "I want to talk to you very seriously, Roy. About Ben."

"I'm very serious," he said.

She sat down on the bed beside him. "Dave Porter says Ben isn't to be trusted."

"Who's Dave Porter?"

"I told you about him—the man I met coming over the pass with those Klikitats. I saw him down at the dock. He was looking for Ben and I said Ben was a business friend. He said to tell you not to trust him."

Roy laughed. "Probably one of Ben's poker victims."

"He said Ben had a bad reputation."

"I don't doubt it. He's a very shady character. An honest man wouldn't be able to swing this deal for me. I 'spect he's going to pocket the lion's share of the bribe money, if the truth were known."

"There's something wrong with Ben's story," Sally said. "I've been thinking about it ever since I saw Dave. It doesn't ring true."

"Who's this Dave?"

178

"I just told you."

"What business he in?"

"He has a claim. That's all I know about him."

"Damned sodbuster."

"Roy, he was trying to warn me."

"Well, I got the money here," Roy said. "Hell of a trip. If Ben and his friend Filler show up with the title, I'll go through with the deal. Haven't any choice."

"I think you ought to see a lawyer. Someone who would know what's going on in the land office."

"No lawyers in Seattle."

"Then talk to Mr. Denny about it."

"Mr. Denny wouldn't approve of bribery," Roy said.

"You wouldn't have to mention bribery. He knows everything that goes on in Olympia, and if the government is going to clamp down on timber cutting, he's probably heard about it. Please, Roy. Sober up and go see him. I'll fix you something to eat."

Roy drew the whisky bottle out of the rucksack and took a long drink.

"Very ingenious scheme," he said. "Sober up so I can talk to Denny. Very ingenious, Sally."

There was no reasoning with him. She went to the kitchen to fix a lunch, knowing he had probably eaten nothing since he started drinking. When she had it ready, Roy had disappeared. He was back in an hour with a gallon jug of whisky.

The rest of the afternoon was a mad scene in which Roy paraded through the house with the jug, haranguing Sally, praising her, trying to make her drink. At last he went upstairs and fell asleep on the bed, a finger hooked through the handle of the jug.

Ben Weller arrived at sunset.

"Hope I'm just in time for supper," he said, when Sally opened the door for him.

"Ben," she said, "Roy's drunk."

Ben's smile faded. "Did he get the money here?"

"Yes."

"Let's be thankful for that."

They went into the living room and sat down.

"Where's Mr. Filler?" Sally said. "Didn't he come with you?"

"He thought it best not to contact Roy himself. But everything went as smooth as silk, Sally. I've got the title."

He drew a paper from his pocket, unfolded it, and passed it to her. "You'll notice it's back-dated ten months. It puts Roy completely in the clear."

The official-looking document was rather convincing, but Sally said, "I'm sorry, Ben. This will have to wait a day or two. I won't take the responsibility of giving you that money while Roy's drunk."

"My god!" Ben exploded. "The thing was settled a week ago. You've no right to shilly-shally now. I've taken a lot of risks to do Roy this favor. You can't leave me out on a limb!"

"Give us till tomorrow," Sally said. "Maybe I can get him sober."

"I've got to get the money to Filler tomorrow." Ben got to his feet and took the title from her. "I'm going to see Roy."

"No!" Sally said sharply, but Ben was already on his way to the stairs. She followed him up and into the bedroom where Roy was asleep. Ben shook him and he woke. After a moment of groaning and staring, he recognized Ben and grasped what was going on. He got up and shook Ben's hand and made a pathetic effort to be businesslike.

"Is Filler here?" he asked.

Ben explained that Filler hadn't come but had got the title, which he handed to Roy.

"Who is this Filler?" Sally demanded. Ben gave her an exasperated glance and she said, "Do you know him, Roy?"

"Never had the pleasure," Roy said. He sat down on the bed and made a show of giving the title his conscientious attention. Sally wondered if he could even make out the words.

"You own three thousand acres of timberland," Ben said pleasantly. "You've owned it for ten months."

Roy laid the paper on the bed beside him. He squinted up at Ben and cocked an eyebrow.

"Ben," Roy said, "Sally says you aren't to be trusted."

Ben faced her and made a stiff little bow. "I regret she has that opinion."

"I heard a bad report about you," Sally said defensively. "I know there's probably nothing to it. Still, it came from someone I happen to respect."

"May I ask who this respected person is? And what he said about me? It's just possible there's a simple explanation."

Sally felt the sarcastic edge to Ben's exaggerated courtesy and she seethed.

"Dave Porter," she said, watching Ben for a reaction and forgetting that Dave had asked not to be mentioned to Ben.

Ben frowned and looked at the floor. "That name means nothing to me."

"You don't know him?"

"No."

"He seemed to know you. He was trying to get in touch with you and I told him you'd be here today."

Sally remembered something then. She said, "Come to think of it, his real name isn't Porter. It's—Partrey. David Partrey."

Ben stared at her. She thought she had never seen anyone turn pale so suddenly. "Partrey?" he said weakly. "Are you sure?"

"Yes. I guess I'm violating a confidence. I've no idea why he changed his name."

"What did he say about me?"

"Nothing specific. Merely that you have a bad reputation."

He was still staring at her, looking as if he didn't believe her. He was a man who could normally conceal his feelings when he wanted to, but now he looked actually sick. He made an effort to laugh.

"Dave Partrey is an old enemy," he said. "I caught him cheating at cards and I called him on it. The other players gave him a beating. He always blamed me. Naturally he'd slander me. I'm surprised he didn't say worse."

This seemed to Sally to be an obvious, spur-of-the-moment lie. To accuse Dave of cheating at cards just didn't ring true.

"When did this happen?" Sally said.

"Last winter aboard the *Norma Jean.* No, it was aboard the *Jenny Platt.* Just a small game, but a man can't put up with cheating."

That clinched it, she thought. Dave wasn't here last winter. And the fact that Ben knew him as Dave Partrey suggested that he had known him back east somewhere. Whatever was between them, Ben wasn't willing to tell the truth about it.

"I don't want anything to do with him," Ben said. "If he comes here, tell him you haven't seen me. Please."

Roy had been listening without interest. Now he looked up at Ben smugly and said, "Sally wants to bring Arthur Denny into this. Says we ought to consult him."

"Denny? She can't be serious."

"Nonsense," Roy agreed. "Utter nonsense."

Ben laughed again, more naturally this time. "Roy, this thing has been hard on my nerves. It wasn't easy to get that title without a cent of cash. You promised the money when I delivered it. For God's sake, give it to me so I can get straightened out with Filler."

"Certainly," Roy said. "I promised payment on delivery and you delivered."

He got up, staggering a little. He crossed to the bureau and stooped to open the drawer where Sally had put the gold-packed saddlebags. Sally moved determinedly in front of him, almost tipping him over backwards. She stood with her back against the bureau so he couldn't open the drawer.

"Not now," she said. "Ben, come in the morning."

"I've got to have that money in Filler's hands tomorrow," Ben said, turning to Roy. "There's no telling what will happen if I don't. That title has been recorded in the land office books and there's no money to cover it. If that's discovered, there'll be hell to pay. Can't you get that through your heads?"

"Wait one hour," Sally said desperately. "Just one hour."

"What difference will that make?" Ben demanded.

"I'll be back in an hour," Sally said.

"She's going to see Denny!" Roy said.

"Never mind what I'm going to do. It certainly won't hurt you to wait an hour, Ben."

She was determined and in the end they agreed to wait, though Ben was exasperated.

"Promise me you won't see Denny," he said.

"I'll promise nothing," Sally said. "You sit down and wait."

She went downstairs and stopped at the desk to scribble a note. She folded it hurriedly and wrote *Dave Porter* on the outside.

In the kitchen, she found the Duwamish cook stoically regarding a dinner that seemed to have been ready for some time. Sally gave her the note.

"Go find Dave Porter," Sally said. She made the squaw repeat the name. "Go to the saloons. Go to Mrs. Bick's boardinghouse and the blacksmith shop and the cookhouse at the mill. Ask in every one of those places. Give him the note and bring him to Arthur Denny's house. If I'm not there, bring him here."

As Sally and the woman hurried through the hall to the front door, Roy and Ben were coming downstairs. Roy was in the lead, painstakingly negotiating the steps. But Sally saw with a gleam of hope that he was not bringing the whisky jug down with him.

"There's food in the kitchen," she called as she went out. "Help yourselves."

Ben's hand was shaking when he picked up the long bone-handled carving knife to slice the venison roast. He served Roy liberally, himself sparingly. He was finding it difficult to think clearly, but he was quite sure there wasn't going to be time to eat much.

He could have coped with Sally's suspicion, if that were the only hitch in his plans. Even if she consulted Arthur Denny, what could Denny say except he knew of no government plan to stop timber-stealing? This would hardly be convincing proof of fraud and Ben could have done something to panic Roy into giving him the money—he could have had him served with a faked summons perhaps, or he could have hired a man to pose as a Department of the Interior investigator. One way or another, he could have put the deal through if it hadn't been for one thing—the name Partrey.

He had almost forgotten that Paul Partrey had a younger brother. Ben was pretty sure the Illinois policeman who had followed him to California had lost the trail there. And he had taken great pains to leave no clues that could be picked up here in Washington. But somehow Partrey had got on to him. And knew he was here tonight!

The only thing now was to get the money and get away at once. It didn't matter how he got it—he probably had only minutes anyway.

He was close to panic. Nothing seemed real and he couldn't think straight. If he could get to Port Townsend, he could get his belongings and the gambling winnings he had buried under the hearth in his cabin. And he could probably get aboard a ship and be on his way to California within a day. There he could get a ship going around the Horn and leave it at Rio or some other South American port. Roy's money would be the foundation for a good life in South America.

The trouble was going to be to get to Port Townsend a day ahead of pursuit. There was no ship here on its way there. He decided to leave town by horseback, headed for Portland. He would hide until his pursuers passed him; then he would double back to the mouth of the Duwamish and hire a canoe from the Indians there. His pursuers would probably go as far as Steilacoom before they realized they had lost him. To further throw them off, he'd hire the canoe to take him to Olympia; then have the crew head for Port Townsend as soon as they were out of the bay. It was a frantic, desperate plan; but if he could make it work, he would gain the time he needed.

They were sitting in silence at the kitchen table.

Roy was nibbling at his food. Ben had eaten nothing. He pushed back his chair and stood up. The money was upstairs in that bureau and it was now or never.

"Roy," he said, "this thing has made a nervous wreck out of me. I'm going up and have a drink of your whisky."

Roy put down his fork. "Bring down the damn jug. I'll have one with you."

Ben strode up the stairs to the bedroom, jerked open the bottom drawer of the bureau, and lifted out the heavy saddlebags. He went to a window and looked out. Twilight was thickening into darkness. Lights shone palely in the windows of the town. The streets were nearly empty.

The window was on the same side of the house as the kitchen but not directly above it. He pushed up the sash and dropped the saddlebags to the ground. Then he picked up the whisky jug and went downstairs.

He found tumblers and poured himself and Roy each two fingers of whisky. He stood by the sink, watching for a chance to slosh his drink down the drain. He knew himself too well to start drinking now. Roy raised his glass.

"Here's to deception and thievery," Roy said.

Ben laughed uneasily. "Damned if I'll drink to that."

Roy regarded him silently, poising his glass but not drinking.

"I'm going to walk down to the dock and back," Ben said. "I need some air. Be right back."

"I'll go along," Roy said.

"Not much. You can't walk ten feet without staggering."

"Here's to a deceiver and a thief," Roy said.

Ben put down his glass. Roy did likewise.

"You chucked my money out the window," Roy said, starting to get up. "I was in the dining room. I saw it go by."

Roy had trouble getting to his feet and Ben hit while he was off balance. Man and chair crashed to the floor. Ben was on top of him, driving his knee into Roy's stomach. He got Roy's left arm between his knees, held the other down with his left hand. His free hand slid inside his vest and came out with a small revolver.

"No!" Roy said. "My God, Ben, let me live."

"I have no choice," Ben said.

He pointed the revolver at Roy's head but didn't fire. He was afraid of the noise. There were no immediate neighbors; still, someone might hear the shot, see Ben leave, and follow. He lowered the hammer and returned the gun to his pocket.

The carving knife lay on the table and he reached it. Roy struggled violently but Ben was fifty pounds heavier and kept him pinned. He slid the knife into Roy under his ribs and upward into his heart. Roy writhed and tried to scream and coughed and died.

Ben quickly washed his hands in a bucket of cold water that was on the sink and dried them on a dish towel. He was dazed now, could hardly remember what he had planned.

He went out and got the saddlebags and walked

toward the waterfront. It was an effort to keep from running. He walked along the skid road past the mill. Three men were loitering in front of the mill. He moved past them knowing he looked pale and wild-eyed and not caring.

He knocked at the door of a cabin with a pasture behind it. He had rented a horse here once before and the man who opened the door remembered him. In ten minutes he was saddled up and ready to go.

He jerked the reins and made the horse act up so that the men in front of the mill would be sure to notice him. He rode a block out of his way to stop a passerby and ask where to pick up the trail that led south to Steilacoom and Olympia and Portland. He knew this perfectly well, but his plan depended on his leaving plenty of clues for the sheriff. He took a last look back and saw a squaw come out of the mill cookhouse and plod along the skid road. It looked like Sally's cook, headed home.

To make sure there would be no doubt which way he had gone, he thundered out of town at a gallop.

19

SEATTLE WAS a lonely encroachment on the wilderness night, a feeble scattering of lights between the bay and the black infinity of the forest. Then, as Dave and Tilluk neared its outskirts, the settlement came quickly alive with lights—open doors, torches, lanterns that jounced through the darkness and converged into a glowing stain at the far edge of town. Dave thought at first there was a meeting or a dance. As they entered the town, it came to him with a shock that the gathering was around Sally's house.

By the time they reached the buildings along the waterfront, the streets were deserted except for a bartender standing by the door of his empty saloon and staring up at the scene of the excitement.

"What happened?" Dave said as they passed the man.

"Somebody knifed Roy Smallwood," the bartender said, glad of a chance to tell the news. "Done for him."

"Who did it?"

"Man named Weller, they say. He skipped."

They ran up the long grade to the house. Somebody had stuck a blazing knot into the ground as if to mark the place. Men and women stood in little clots around the yard and on the porch, their faces pale and stern. Children stood close to their parents. A light shone from every room in the house and shadows constantly crossed the windows.

A large, hatless man guarded the front door, but he made only a halfhearted effort to stop Dave and Tilluk from going in. "It's a mess in there," he said as they pushed past.

Half a dozen men were in the kitchen, standing in shocked fascination around a corpse with the bone handle of a carving knife sticking out of it. Dave went into the living room, where people stood and stared at Sally, who sat on the sofa, looking straight ahead. A woman knelt beside her, holding her hand, talking in a soothing tone. Dave spoke her name. She looked up at him dazedly and didn't recognize him until he went over and placed a hand on her shoulder and shook her gently.

"You," she said. "You're too late."

"She's coming out of it,' somebody said.

Dave didn't know what to say except to ask stupidly if there was anything he could do for her. She smiled faintly and shook her head.

The sheriff came in from the kitchen, a lank, hollow-cheeked man with tobacco-stained lips.

"I guess I got it halfway straight now," he said. "Seems this Weller killed him and took two saddlebags full of money you had in the house. He rented a horse from John Pray and he asked Lee Terry how to get to the south trail. Only thing I don't know is what this Weller looks like. Could you tell me, Mrs. Smallwood?"

"I can," Dave said and gave a description of Ben Weller. He added, "His real name is Bart Hadder.

He was convicted of murder in Illinois and escaped." He told the sheriff of his long search then.

"I'm going to summon a posse," the sheriff said. "I've already sent two men for horses. I reckon you'd like to go along."

"Can you take this man, too?" Dave nodded to Tilluk.

"A siwash? Well, yes. He'll be useful at tracking."

They went out in the yard and the sheriff picked three other possemen. When he lined them up to deputize them, he carefully made Tilluk stand aside. "Law don't allow Injun deputies," he said.

While they were waiting for the horses, Dave went back into the house to see that Sally was taken care of. Two of the women said they were going to stay the rest of the night with her. Then Dave suggested that some of the men get the body out of the house.

"No," Sally said. "Take it up and lay it on the bed. I want him here till he's buried. I want him in his own house."

The sheriff came in and said the horses were outside. To Sally, he said, "We'll get Weller, ma'am. We'll get him by morning."

Sally shook her head as if to clear it. "It doesn't matter. Roy's dead."

"Weller's a mad dog," Dave said. "He has no right to live."

"Poor Ben," Sally said.

They looked at her in amazement. She didn't know what she was saying, Dave thought. Then he saw this wasn't so. She had been brutally shocked, but she was calm and rational. And she was taking a fatalistic view of the tragedy that was beyond the grasp of the rest of them.

"You try to get some rest, ma'am," the sheriff said.

Ma'am, Dave thought. *She is a very great lady and he instinctively calls her ma'am.*

They galloped down the skid road and up again and out of town, slowing the horses as soon as they reached the woods. Tilluk led the way along the trail that wove darkly and treacherously among close-growing firs. From time to time he stopped and got off his horse to study the ground. He pointed out that Weller's horse had one barred shoe—which would greatly simplify the business of following him if the trail became confused by other fresh shoe marks.

They came to the Duwamish about a mile above the mouth. Here the trail merged with another that wound along the bank. It was easier to follow here because the light was better, but it was dangerously scarred with drainage cuts, cave-ins and protruding roots. They drove ahead in a long file, riding at a canter when they could, winding through the forest as through a mad dream. Before they had gone five miles, a horse went down with a broken leg. His bruised rider reluctantly shot him and turned back on foot. The sheriff ordered Tilluk to set a more cautious pace.

Dave puzzled about Weller's plans. If he was going all the way to Portland, he would no doubt stop at Steilacoom or Olympia for a fresh horse and supplies, in which case there was a good chance of overtaking him before he could get on the road again. Remembering the cabin and the packed luggage at Port Townsend, Dave wondered if perhaps he planned to take a ship or a canoe back there. If the posse didn't lose the track, they would surely reach him before he could sail. *If* they didn't lose the track. Weller's best, if not his only chance was to see that they lost it.

An hour after midnight, they reached the junction of the trail with the Steilacoom road. Much to everyone's surprise, Weller's tracks turned left here—toward the new road over the Naches pass. Tilluk halted them, keeping them back until he had a chance to examine the ground carefully. Then he waved them on, toward the pass, but after a couple of hundred yards the tracks vanished.

One of the men had brought a lantern and he lighted it. Tilluk pointed to the mark of a horseshoe near the side of the road that had been partly obliterated by a bootmark. The horse that made it had been going in the opposite direction. Tilluk led them back to the junction, then went ahead on foot. Before long the barred shoe prints showed up again, headed for Steilacoom.

"Cagy," the sheriff said. "He rode toward the pass, then rode back past the junction and tied his horse. Then he walked back and kicked out all the tracks except those that led toward the pass. He figured we'd ride hell-bent toward the pass without looking for tracks, once we'd seen he turned that way. Well, he just lost that much time. Let's hightail it for Steilacoom."

"Wait," Dave said, swinging down from his horse. "There's that bootmark again. He could have done the same thing again—doubled back toward Seattle and walked back and covered his tracks. Then he could have hid in the woods till we passed."

"Poppycock!" the sheriff said. "He wouldn't dare go back. The town would lynch him."

"He could go to Sealth's Indians and hire a canoe. They probably won't hear of the killing until late in the morning."

"Well, yes," the sheriff admitted. "But it seems to me you're making something out of nothing."

"He's got to gain time. If he can trick us into going on to Steilacoom while he's riding the other way toward Elliot Bay, he'll be at least a day ahead of us."

"Well, yes. But the tracks point to Steilacoom."

"They'll peter out soon enough. The rest of you go ahead, but watch the tracks. When they stop, turn back. I'm turning right now."

"If you find tracks on the trail headed the other way, fire your rifle," the sheriff said.

Dave rode back to the junction and dismounted and peered at the ground. There were bootprints as far as the junction but none on the trail to Seattle, no sign that hoofmarks had been erased there. Then he saw that the bootprints led into the woods and he had a tense moment. If Weller had gone into the woods here to wait for the posse to pass, it was possible that he was still there. He might be watching Dave that moment, might have him in his sights. The other possibility was that he had worked his way through the woods, paralleling the trail so as to leave no tracks. The going would be slow and murderously rough, but a desperate man might get through by leading his horse.

If Weller was in there waiting, it would be suicide to go in. Dave led his horse down the trail. It was so dark that he sometimes had to stop and kneel in order to see the ground clearly. He rounded a bend and found the barred shoe mark again, coming out of the woods and pointing toward Seattle. He fired his rifle in the air, reloaded, swung onto his horse and kicked the animal into a lope.

He rode as hard as he dared, stopping to check the tracks now and then to be sure Weller hadn't left the trail again. He lost all sense of time, had no idea how far he had come. He had reached that stage of exhaustion where his mind seemed only tenuously related to his body and perceptions reached it slowly and inexact. He had a persistent impression that the trail led in a great circle and that he was making the same turns, dodging the same branches again and again.

Just before dawn, he got a glimpse of his man. The trail had wound up a ridge away from the Duwamish, and there was a brief view of the country below with the silver line of the river bent through the forest. Weller was fording the stream a mile ahead—a vague shape that emerged from one black shore and was soon absorbed by the other.

Dave put down an impulse to push his tired horse ruthlessly. There was no sense in risking a fall or a ridden-down horse at this stage. If he didn't catch Weller on the trail, he'd overtake him easily enough at Sealth's camp before he could recruit a crew and shove off. For that was surely where Weller was headed—it was the only possibility left.

When he reached the ford, Dave let his horse drink a little. He listened for the hoofbeats of the posse and once he thought he heard them faintly but he wasn't sure. He wondered if the sheriff had stubbornly gone on to Steilacoom after all.

An hour later, near the place where the trail branched toward Seattle, he rounded a bend and saw Weller a stone's throw ahead. The big man was riding bent stiffly forward as if he was saddle-sore. He turned, saw Dave, wheeled his horse around and waited.

He isn't sure about me, Dave thought. He doesn't know if I'm from the posse or just a traveler on the way to Seattle.

"You're up early!" Weller called cheerfully.

Dave made no reply. Here was the man who had killed Paul—the man he had sought vainly for so long, lain in wait for, followed across the Sound and back. Here at last was Ben Weller, waiting for him, and there was nothing to be gained by putting on a mask of friendliness. Now at last it was take him or kill him or be killed. Weller's hand slid inside his coat.

Dave reined his horse to a stop twenty-five feet away and dismounted, seeing the bewilderment in the other's face. Weller no doubt had a revolver and the edge would be his at closer range. And a rifle is an awkward weapon when your aim depends upon a horse's whim. Dave had only one shot to fire and he had to be in a position to make it count. He jerked up the rifle and said, "Point your horse to my left and get off. One false move and you're dead."

The glint of the revolver, the flash of the shot, and the whir of the bullet past Dave's ear seemed simultaneous. Weller's horse shied. His left hand crossed his right, cocking the gun. He got off another snap shot that went wild. He swung his horse all the way around and raised the small revolver for a third try. He took time to aim now, matching Dave's calmness, but he never got off the shot.

Dave had him squarely in his sights and he fired. Weller went weak and loose and dropped the revolver and slumped forward over the horse's neck. Strangely, something inside Dave snapped and for an instant he went weak and loose too. Weller's horse turned toward Seattle and started off leisurely. Weller rallied and urge the animal into a gallop.

Dave picked up the revolver and pocketed it. He reloaded the rifle, pulled himself into the saddle, and stolidly resumed the chase.

Weller was plainly badly hurt. He rode limply, his head down, his heels pounding his horse's flanks. He didn't see the fork in the trail—or he no longer cared—and his horse took the branch to Seattle instead of bearing to the left toward the Duwamish camp.

Dave slowly reduced the distance between them and was a few yards behind when they reached the skid road. A ragged edge of fog reached out from the bay to smear the low part of the settlement and make bleak hulks of the buildings along the waterfront. When they had passed the mill, Weller reined his horse to a sudden stop and Dave overshot him, halting his horse a few lengths beyond.

Weller half fell out of the saddle, pulled off the saddlebags, and stumbled toward a vacant lot between two log buildings. He sank to his hands and knees, got up, staggered on into the lot, and sank down again. After a moment he rolled over on his back and lay still. Dave walked over and stood over him.

"You got me through the lungs," Weller said.

Dave picked up the heavy saddlebags, laid them aside, and knelt over Weller. The man's clothing was soaked with blood and there was a crust of blood on his lips and chin. He was breathing in gasps.

"Not much I can do for you," Dave said.

A man and woman burst out of a cabin in back of the lot and ran toward them. The woman wore an overcoat over a nightgown and her hair hung down her back in braids. The man slipped his arms through his suspenders as he came.

"Is this the man stabbed Smallwood?" he asked excitedly.

Dave nodded.

"Why don't you finish the fiend?" the woman demanded.

"Where's the jail?" Dave said.

"Give me that gun and, by God, I'll finish him," the woman said. She stepped close to Weller and spat at his face. Dave jerked her away.

"You keep your hands off my wife!" the man said. The woman moved close to Weller again and Dave caught her by the arm and spun her around and sat her on the ground.

"I told you—" the man began.

"You keep her away from him," Dave said softly, "or I'll kick her tail back to your cabin. Now I want an answer to my question. Where's the jail?"

"It's a block over and up—on the back end of Marker's barn. You can't see it for the fog."

"Get up," Dave said to Weller.

Weller got slowly to his feet, staggered two steps, and collapsed.

"I've got no strength," he gasped. "I'm suffocating slowly."

There was the chop of hoofs up the skid road and Dave turned and tried to see up the street. In a moment, the sheriff and his men rode ghostlike out of the mist.

"Is the bastard still alive?" the sheriff said, riding into the vacant lot and dismounting.

"He's dying," Dave said.

"Well, I told Mrs. Smallwood we'd have him by morning," the sheriff said with satisfaction. "You get the money?"

He saw the saddlebags and picked them up. Dave let their weight answer his question.

The sheriff stood over Weller and said, "You can

lay right there and die. I'm damned if I'll do anything for you. Roy Smallwood was a friend of mine."

"We ought to get him to the jail," Dave said. "And he ought to have a doctor. He's likely to hang on a while."

"No doctor in Seattle," the sheriff said. He turned to one of the possemen. "Griggs, you sit in front of that cabin and guard him. Don't go near him and don't let anybody else go near him. If he gets up, shoot his legs out from under him."

Other citizens were crowding up now, most of them half dressed. The sheriff herded them all out of the lot. They seemed fully in accord with his plan to leave Weller alone to die.

"He did cruel and he'll get cruel," the sheriff said. "We'll leave him suffer for the whole town to see."

Dave didn't like it. Whatever cruelty Ben Weller deserved, there was nothing to be gained by making a display of his agony, making the most of the ugliness of his death. Well, it was up to the sheriff, he thought, and he said nothing.

He and the sheriff took the money up to Sally then, finding her at breakfast with the two women who had stayed with her. She looked drawn and hollow-eyed but was perfectly composed. The sheriff gave her a brief report of the chase and told her that Ben was dying, but didn't mention that he had been left in the middle of a vacant lot.

She seemed relieved that the money was safe, but she didn't want it in the house and asked Dave to take it to Low and Terry's store and put it in their big iron safe.

Before he left, he said, "You're taking this well. I admire you."

"Roy was my whole life," she said. "But I'm not going to cry out against the way of things. That would be blasphemous."

He walked back to the waterfront with the sheriff, marveling at her. They took the money into the store and J. N. Low opened each roll of gold coins, counted them, and gave Dave a receipt. The sheriff left him then, and Dave strolled back to the lot where Weller lay.

The street had come to life now. Men moved in and out of the stores, raised their hats to women with baskets on their arms. Indians unloaded bags of potatoes and barrels of fish from wagons at the dock. Oxen skidded logs to the mill. Passers-by paused to gape at the dying man. No one went near him.

Tilluk was sitting on a cabin step with Weller's guard, and Dave beckoned to him and went into the lot. Weller lay on his back with his arms folded across his chest and his eyes open, blinking up at the hazy sky. He smiled faintly.

"I've been trying to die," he said. "It comes slow."

Dave helped Weller to his feet. He and Tilluk made a seat of their hands and began to carry the big man toward the jail. The guard made no protest; but before they were out of the lot, the sheriff ran up and blocked their way.

"You heard my orders to leave him lay!" he shouted.

"Get out of the way," Dave said.

The sheriff turned to the little group of onlookers that had gathered. "You folks give me a hand. Make them put that prisoner down."

Dave straightened, leaving Weller leaning on Tilluk.

"You people are trying to build a town here," he said, "a little spot of civilization in a savage country. Now you have a choice. Are you going to act like civilized people or like savages?"

He bent to pick up Weller again. No one moved to stop him.

"He's right," Lee Terry, who had been in the posse, said. "Let them do what they can for the man."

"You listen to me!" the sheriff snapped.

"If we'd listened to you on the trail last night, we'd be in Steilacoom now and Weller as free as a bird," Terry said.

Somebody laughed. Withered, the sheriff made no further interference. They carried Weller to the lean-to that served as a jail and laid him on a cot. Dave loosened his clothing, bandaged him with a towel, brought him water.

"You're Partrey," Weller said. "Paul Partrey's brother. I'm surprised you'd do this for me."

"I'm a little surprised myself," Dave admitted.

"I have about six hundred dollars buried under the hearth of a cabin near Port Townsend. I'd like you to have it. I'll tell you how to find the cabin."

"I've been there."

Weller smiled ironically, staring up at the whitewashed boards of the low ceiling. "You'd have got me eventually, wouldn't you? One way or another."

"Why don't you leave that money to Ike Covey?"

"You've been to the Covey farm too?"

"He could use it."

"It's yours and anything else of value you find. Do what you like with it. You witness that, Sheriff. I'm making the man who killed me my heir."

He fell silent then and after a while sank into a gasping sleep and died.

20

DAVE WENT HOME with Lee Terry, ate a huge breakfast, and slept most of the day. The next morning he attended Roy Smallwood's funeral in a newly cleared cemetery studded with more stumps than headstones. Then, having borrowed money from Terry, he hired a Duwamish canoe and made the two-day trip to Port Townsend.

He found Stephen and his brother at their roadside shacks and took them with him to Weller's cabin. Opening the lock with Weller's key, he went in, tore up the hearth, and uncovered a cigar box with six hundred and twenty dollars in it. With the Indians' help, he loaded Weller's possessions into a hired wagon and took them into town. He kept a shotgun and revolver from Ben's arsenal and sold the rest of the stuff to a merchant for another ninety dollars.

Two days later he was back in Seattle, where Tilluk was waiting after having been to the Puyallup valley and to Steilacoom to get their horses. Before they left town, Dave called on Sally. They talked a long time, casually and without strain, and he again marveled at her lack of bitterness.

"Everything's out of perspective," she said, "but in a general way I've been trying to make plans. I'll have the mill and the house and the money Roy left;

so I won't have to worry about my living. But that isn't enough. I want to do something with my life besides just live it out.

"I've been thinking about the Indians here. They'll be pushed off the land, herded into reservations—and slowly destroyed. There's no help for it. They can't fight back and they can't fit themselves into the white man's civilization. But I've been thinking about the children. If they could learn to speak English and to read and write and figure, maybe life would be a little easier for them. So I'm going to teach at least a few of them. I'm going to start a school for Indian children. Does that sound completely crazy?"

Dave smiled. "It sounds like a nerve-racking job. But you could do it. And it would be a fine thing. There'd be a lot of satisfaction in it."

After a moment, he said, "You know, I think I learned something on that ship. When I came to, I was in a filthy black hole and it was like being dead. It seemed to me that all that was left of me was the life I *had* lived. Nothing I had ever done or thought was dead; it was still going on—all at once and forever."

Sally looked mildly alarmed. "It's strange that you should say that, because I've been thinking the same thing. The life Roy and I had together isn't over. Somehow, somewhere, it's still going on—all at once and forever, as you say. It's a good thought."

"It wasn't for me," he said, grinning and getting

up to leave. "My life looked selfish and lonely and meaningless. I didn't much care if it went on or not. A life ought to be part of something."

"It ought to have a meaning in relation to other lives," Sally said. She had gone to the door with him and she gave him her hand. She said, "What are you going to do now?"

"I don't know. I'm a little worried about it."

"I'm not," she said, smiling. "You'll be all right."

He went away thinking that he had called on her to say something encouraging and he had left with her saying it to him.

He spent the rest of the day in the saddle, reaching the turn-off to his claim at twilight and sending Tilluk there while he rode on to Fort Steilacoom. He found Captain Maloney at his quarters and they spent half the night talking.

"I had a sergeant waiting to meet you on the Steilacoom road the morning of the fifteenth," the captain said when Dave had told him about being shanghaied. "When he came back without seeing you, I figured you were in some kind of trouble; but I didn't know where to start looking for you . . . Well, I've been laying for that Holland Gay. I know he sells whisky to the Indians, but he always has somebody else do his dirty work and I never could get anything on him. Now we've got him."

"Do you suppose he knows I got off that ship?" Dave said.

"I doubt it. The Weller affair is known all over the Sound, but the details are all mixed up. As I heard the story, he was killed by a posse—with no names mentioned. I tried to find out if you were in on it and couldn't."

"Fine," Dave said, grinning. "Let's map a campaign."

The Covey family was at breakfast and didn't see Dave ride up with Weller's cigar box under his arm. He could hear them in the kitchen and he pushed open the door without knocking, unprepared for the surprise his appearance would cause. They were all at the table—Ann, her father, and the two younger children—and for a moment they just sat and looked. Then Ike Covey got up with his usual hearty greeting on his lips.

"It's a pleasure to know we was misinformed," he said. "We heard you had gone back to the States."

Dave joined them at a breakfast of fatback, eggs and gingerbread, eating with the heavy cigar box on his lap. Ann was completely silent, but he could feel her eyes on him.

" 'Bout a week ago there was a soldier here, a sergeant," Ike Covey said. "He'd been sent to meet you and ride to Seattle with you and you hadn't showed up. Ann showed him the way to your claim and you wasn't there. We was sort of worried for a while, then Holland told us he seen you board a ship headed around the Horn."

"Holland is a liar," Dave said. "You ought to know that by now."

Ann's chin went out, anger flared in her eyes, and Dave realized he was getting off to a bad start. He grinned at her and seemed only to increase her antagonism.

She said, "Ella, take the teakettle to the pump and fill it." When the little girl had gone out, Ann said icily, "We heard about Uncle Ben. Ella doesn't know what he did or how he died. We thought you were gone and couldn't be in the posse that killed him. But I guess you were."

Dave put down his fork and met her eyes. "You might as well hear it from me. I killed him."

"I guess you're real proud of yourself!"

He glanced from one solemn face to another. The grim bewilderment in twelve-year-old Bobby's eyes was something he would always remember.

"I'd like you to know how it was. I overtook him on the trail. He was blazing away at me with a revolver when I shot him. He rode on into Seattle and died a few hours later."

Ike Covey cleared his throat. Looking from Bobby to Dave, he said, "He was a bad man. Crazy, I guess. I reckon a lot of folks goes crazy over money, only he was worse 'n most. We bear you no grudge."

Dave set the cigar box in front of Ike. "Ben left this. There's about six hundred dollars there. It's yours."

Ike Covey opened the box and took out a roll of

coins and unwrapped it. The bright gold spilled into his hand. He quickly wrapped the money again and put it back into the box as if it were something to be enjoyed in small doses.

Dave got up from the table without looking at Ann, not wanting this to seem a thing aimed at her. *I mustn't act as if I know this money will set her free,* he thought. *Let her decide for herself to be free.*

No one had spoken since he placed the box in front of Ike. Now Bobby voiced what they were all thinking.

"That'll pay off Holland," he said happily.

Dave opened the door and paused. "Pay him right away, Ike. Go into Steilacoom and do it this morning."

"Yes," Ike Covey said. "I'll do that. I'll sure do that."

"And do me a favor. Don't tell Holland I'm back."

"It'll be a pleasure not to say nothin'."

Ann got up and came around the table, trying to be very casual, but he looked at her closely now and saw her restraint and her happiness shining through it. She said, "Thank you, David," and gave him her hand—rather formally, he thought.

The platoon stacked arms and stood at ease while a lieutenant and a sergeant went into Gay's saloon and herded the occupants, including Holland, into the street. A detail of four soldiers then went inside with the sergeant and smashed every jug, bottle and barrel in the place. Next, ropes were fastened to log ends and the building was joyously collapsed. Finally, in orderly military fashion, four men to a log, the remains were chucked into Steilacoom Bay.

An hour later Holland Gay and his lawyer were at Fort Steilacoom, sitting across a table from Captain Maloney. The lawyer, a middle-aged Irishman as small and peppery as Maloney was stolid, slapped the table and bellowed about military high-handedness.

"Calm down, O'Hara," the captain said. "I had authority for what I did!"

"Authority! What authority?"

Maloney slid a paper across the table. "That's an order, issued at the request of the new governor, to stop the sale of whisky to Indians. It specifically states that I am to destroy all liquor, buildings and equipment used by offenders."

"I ain't no offender," Holland protested in a martyrlike voice. He was flushed and nervous and had neglected to take off his hat—a discourtesy that gave a superlative aspect to Maloney's dislike of him. "I had a man on Fox Island makin' whisky for me. How'd I know he was sellin' it to the poor Injuns?"

"I have an Indian who'll testify he bought whisky at the back door of your saloon."

"Injuns lie."

"They'll testify to anything," O'Hara said. "But even if you had a case, Mike Maloney, you had no right to destroy Mr. Gay's property until he was proved guilty. Most arrogant thing I ever heard of!

And you'll pay through the nose for it, I promise you. I'll see to it!"

Maloney got up from the table and went over to a desk and got a cigar and bit off the end. He came back and stood over the two men and made a little speech.

"You know how it is in a new territory, O'Hara. The processes of democratic government haven't had a chance to develop. A lot of responsibility falls on the military. Now think a minute. Remember when that whole band of Snohomish got drunk and attacked Fort Nisqually? Remember the settler and his wife and two children who were murdered by drunken Puyallups last year? Remember the sawyer who was pushed into his saw by a drunken Indian and lost his arm? And you know as well as I do that all summer whole camps of Nisquallies have been getting liquored up and having war dances."

O'Hara slapped the table again. "Nobody's trying to tell you liquor's a good thing for Indians! The point is you've no right to judge a man. That's for the court to do."

"The point is that I'm going to put Gay out of business!" Maloney said, letting his voice go now. "And I'm going to do it as quickly and effectively as possible."

"I meant to get outen the liquor business," Holland said. "I had a buyer all lined up for the saloon. And you come along and throwed it in the bay!"

"You know what you're going to get out of, Gay?" Maloney said. "You're going to get out of

Washington Territory. For good. If you don't, you're going to jail."

"Bluff!" O'Hara said. "Military bluff! You have no case."

Maloney held a match to his cigar and puffed assiduously to get it going. "O'Hara, your client hasn't told you about another sideline of his—shanghaing sailors. On the fourteenth of this month he slugged one David Partrey and turned him over to the mate of the *Amy Lester*. And don't tell me I can't prove it. I've got a case that will get him two years in the pen."

Holland looked sick. He muttered, "It's a lie. How do I know what my bartenders might do?"

"Shut up!" O'Hara snapped.

"I'll give him a week to sell out, pack up and get out," Maloney said.

Holland started to speak and had to clear his throat and start over. "He ain't got no case. This Partrey went back to the States."

Captain Maloney went to the door and jerked it open. In a moment, Dave came in. Holland blinked unbelievingly.

"Mr. O'Hara, meet Mr. Partrey."

"What's all this nonsense about shanghaing?" O'Hara said weakly, his confidence gone.

Dave briefly told his story, his eyes on Holland, who looked like a man with a fever. Beads of sweat formed under his hatbrim, grew, burst, and ran down his cheeks, which were the color of baked salmon. Once or twice he started a halfhearted protest, but O'Hara glared him into silence.

213

"You see, O'Hara?" the captain said. "There's more to this than bluff."

O'Hara studied Holland. He said, "They've got you like a chicken in a bag."

Holland wiped his face with his sleeve. "It's all a dirty lie they made up. It's military bluff and high-handedness, that's what it is."

"Frankly," Maloney said to O'Hara, "I'd rather have your client out of the Territory for good than in the pen for a couple of years. So I'm giving him a chance to pack up and get."

"And I advise him to take it!" O'Hara said, slapping the table in front of Gay. The lawyer got up and strode out of the room. Holland looked around uncertainly and followed.

"One week!" Maloney called after him. "If you're not gone by then, you'll go to the pen!" He turned to Dave. "High-handed, am I? Well, a soldier has to be a little high-handed."

"You don't know it," Dave grinned, "but you just helped a pretty girl break her engagement."

The captain threw Dave an inquiring glance but said nothing. There was a knock on the door and a corporal came in, saluted casually, and proffered a folded paper.

"Message from Lieutenant Latham, sir. That wagon train finally got over the hump."

Maloney took the paper and sighed noisily. "Eighteen days. It took them eighteen days to get up the Yakima and the Naches and over the summit of the pass. Had to cut their own road part of the way. Had to improve the road the citizens built. Had to let their wagons over a cliff with ropes. Lost two wagons . . ."

"Where are they now?" Dave asked, turning to the corporal.

"It's hard to say, the way them oxen travel. But if they don't have no more bad luck, they ought to reach the Puyallup valley in a day or two."

21

IT WAS A WARM October day and an undeclared holiday for the settlers around Steilacoom, most of whom loaded their families into wagons and drove out to meet the immigrant party. Not wanting to strain their teams on a steep grade, the spectators gathered at a little meadow at the base of Elhi Hill where the road cascaded out of the woods. They left their animals to graze and lined the road and waited.

Dave tied his horse and joined Lafayette Balch and Dr. Tolmie, the Hudson's Bay factor who was officially antagonistic to settlers and personally fond of them. Having heard that the train was low on food, the hard-bitten old doctor had thrown a beef and a hundred-pound bag of flour into his wagon.

"They say there are nearly two hundred people in this party," Balch said to Dave. "It ought to be easy to sell your claim to one of them."

Dave took a deep breath and let it out, then he grinned. He said, "No chance. I've changed my mind."

"You're staying?"

"A man would be a fool to leave Washington just when it's beginning to open up."

Balch clapped him on the shoulder. "Of course he would. Why, there's a chance to make a fortune if you plan right."

Dave looked straight ahead across the clearing with the wagons parked in it and the tall trees rising in a sea behind it. And looked over the trees to the blue foothills and the great white mountain that was so unbelievable and so real and that the Indians said was God.

"And there's another kind of chance," Dr. Tolmie said. "A chance to be part of something big, to help develop a new community. Some things will come quickly now—schools, churches, new roads, reservations for the Indians. Others will take years. You could spend the rest of your life growing with the country and helping it grow. It would be a life well spent."

"Yes," Dave said.

"There's a road in now," Balch said. "The settlements will grow into towns. The next thing will be a railroad that will make cities out of the towns. Guess where they'll be and you'll get rich. I'm betting on Steilacoom."

"I'll take Commencement Bay," the doctor said. "It's a natural place for a city."

"The cities will be where the best harbors are," Dave said.

"They'll be where the energetic men are," Balch said.

The Covey wagon rolled up the road then with Ann and Ella sharing the seat with their father, and Bobby standing behind them. They jolted into the clearing and climbed down and found a place at the edge of the road. Ann was a study in supple grace and for a moment every eye was upon her. She wore a flowing green riding dress that contrasted prettily with the deep brown of her eyes and her coronet of blond braids. She saw Dave at once and smiled and waved, and heads turned to see whom she was waving at.

He grinned and waved back. He had stayed away from her the last two days because he had wanted her to break with Holland in her own way—without her feeling that he was pressing her to get it over with. He had seen Holland's horse in the Covey pasture the afternoon before and he supposed that Holland was making a last pathetic bid for her, asking her to go away with him. At suppertime he had had another look and the horse was gone—a good sign, he thought.

"There's a lass wants your company," Dr. Tolmie said, winking at Balch. "What are you waiting for?"

"How can you tell?" Dave grinned.

"I've a degree in biology," the doctor said, "and a lifetime devoted to the independent study of the subject."

"You'd better be right," Dave muttered, leaving to join the Coveys.

Ike offered his customary handshake and Bobby came up to shake hands, too, as if this were his spontaneous way of saying Dave was forgiven for killing Uncle Ben.

Ike Covey was in a trance.

"The first train over the pass!" he said. "It will be a great thing to see. A historical thing."

"It will be something for Dave to tell about when he gets back to Illinois," Ann said.

It was more a question than a statement and their eyes met. He saw then that the strain between them was almost gone. He knew somehow that she had broken cleanly with Holland and he knew it for sure. She would tell him about it some day when she felt like it; there was no hurry. And she perhaps knew in the same mysterious way that he was not going back to Illinois. Dr. Tolmie was a good biologist.

Yet there was a vestige of uncertainty to be erased and he said, "Yes—I'll tell it the minute I step off the train."

No one said anything for a moment. Then Ann frowned. "The train?"

"I figure I'll go back to Illinois for a visit when I can travel on a train," he said. "That'll be fifteen years. Maybe twenty."

"It won't be that long!" Ike Covey said, though neither of them heard him. "Why, it won't be ten. We'll be standin' alongside a railroad track like alongside this here road, waitin' for that old engine to come a-puffin' out of the mountains . . ."

Ike suddenly held up his hand and said "Shush!"—as if someone else were talking. "Listen. It's the wagon party!"

Dave heard it then, the creak and rumble of wagons swaying down the hill, still hidden by the forest. And he saw the excitement in Ann's eyes and she moved closer to him.

And then the tired and battered train came slowly out of the woods and down the hill toward them.

Old Asher Sergeant led the column on a lame stallion that had once been a fine horse. His hair and beard were white against cheeks burned to the color of his saddle and he rode ramrod straight with a rifle cradled in his arms. After him came the wagons, other horsemen, and men, women and children on foot—walking to spare the oxen. Lame, weak, dazed, they came, nodding howdy-do to the valley folks and saying the soil looked fine.

And they rolled and rattled and trudged into the valley. A hundred and eighty people. Sixty families from Illinois, Indiana, Kentucky, Missouri. Sometimes their names were scrawled on wagon covers with axle grease. Names like Baker, Bonney, Downey, Kincaid, Judson, Lane, Longmire, Wright, Woolery. Names that were new to the country and would become old to it. Names that would be given to towns and farms and schools and businesses. To children and grandchildren.

And the valley folks wanted to cheer and choked up and clapped their hands instead. And Dave found he was holding Ann's hand and he saw that her chin was stuck out mysteriously and saw the tears in her eyes and the pride and felt his own throat tighten.

And the old leader waved jauntily and his old horse pulled up his head and danced and tried to single-foot, headed straight for Steilacoom.